AP164: Ábalos&Herreros

selected by
Kersten Geers and David Van Severen
Juan José Castellón González
Florian Idenburg and Jing Liu
with an interpretation in photographs by
Stefano Graziani

CCA PARK BOOKS

ABA-06

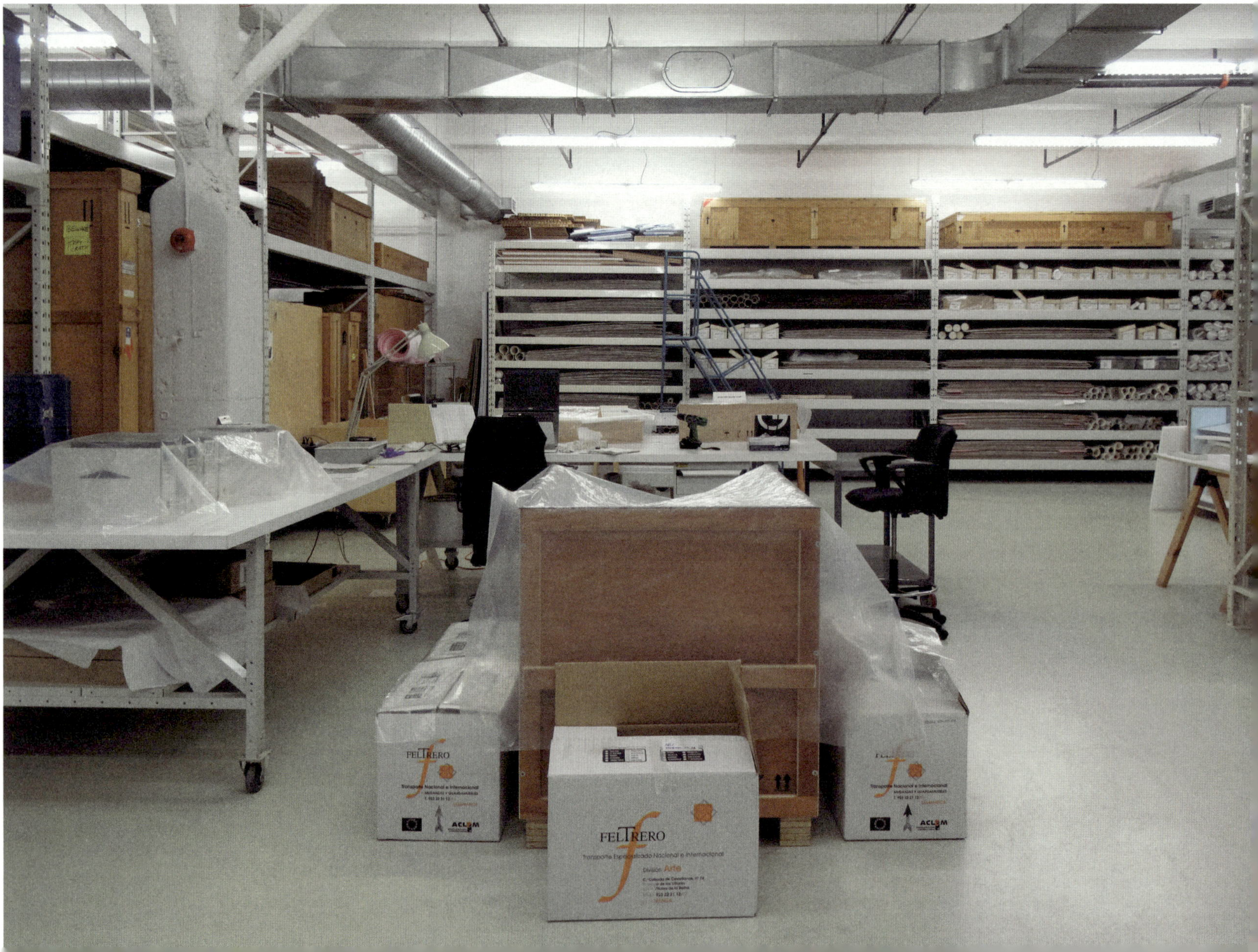

Iñaki Ábalos and Juan Herreros
8   A Conversation

Giovanna Borasi
22 Out of the Box: Ábalos&Herreros

Stefano Graziani
28 Proofs of Relevance

Kersten Geers and David Van Severen
52 November 2014
58 Industrial Architecture
91 March 2015

Juan José Castellón González
98 October 2014
104 Jai Tech
139 May 2015

Florian Idenburg and Jing Liu
144 October 2014
150 Landscapes of the Hyperreal
187 July 2015

Iñaki Ábalos
198 September 2015

Juan Herreros
199 September 2015

202 Archive description and list of projects

A Conversation
Iñaki Ábalos and Juan Herreros

1993. 09
M.MANSILLA, ROJO, TUÑON.

CIRCO

UNA CONVERSACION.
IÑAKI ABALOS, JUAN HERREROS.

Iñaki Ábalos and Juan Herreros

We see the purpose of these *CIRCO*s as being to create a forum for conversation. Crafting such places, spaces made of words, is a luxury for print media as well as for architecture, as this is truly a built place, especially if we are capable of making it a space where ideas can easily flow. It would be a shame to make it rigid, to make us think upon receiving it (and this is a real danger): "Heavens, another dreary diatribe by someone with an axe to grind." These letters from the editors of *CIRCO* are practically the only ones we exchange with our friends, so we've decided to try to turn their idea into a comfortable, liveable place.

We'll start with an inconsequential fact related to the idea of conversation between friends. Someone (rather clumsily) asked us whether, as we both sign the texts, we write them together, and how we could do that. Our answer—"exactly like our projects"—was, to tell the truth, just as inconsequential as the conversation, or at least that was what we thought until we were faced with the opposite question: how do we design our projects? (Actually it was more general, "how to design projects," but this question only turns into a question once translated). We had to say it, and say it to ourselves: exactly the way we write, like a conversation.

So, conversing about conversation is the pirouette we aim to perform in this circus meeting place that has no physical presence. Conversation is the way in which things take shape

Asi que conversar sobre la conversación es la pirueta que queremos hacer en este lugar circense de encuentro sin presencia física. La conversación es el modo en el que las cosas se forman en nuestra mano, en nuestro cerebro, en nuestro ojo: mediante una conversación ya vieja, larga, casi permanente, entre nosotros, de cada uno consigo mismo, con los demás arquitectos, con los demás demases: como un fluido que avanza y mantiene una trayectoria relativamente errática, salta inopinadamente, vuelve y describe trayectorias muy diferenciadas: no solo círculos o espirales, también figuras aleatorias, lentas y torpes o a ratos rapidísimas, vectoriales como flechas. Pero no es la geometría (simbólica) de las trayectorias lo importante sino resaltar que no importa ni el origen ni el destino sino el propio fluir, que fluya, que se mueva, la movilidad, el placer del viaje físico o mental, transportarse.

Al hablar las cosas se consumen y aparecen otras nuevas: la conversación es ese avanzar, dejar unos temas y empezar otros, describir trayectorias, hacer viajes en la mente. Existe una arquitectura así, hecha de "capturas" -en lenguaje de Soriano, otro sofista-, mezclas instántaneas, apaños, jirones, mezclas explosivas, sobre todo mezclas que siempre pasan desapercibidas a los profesionales del comentario (el comentario es lo contrario de la conversación).

Al citar la conversación como origen del proyecto salta Rorty en la cabeza, la analogía de la filosofía como conversación que él defiende, tan parecida a un apego al saber ensayístico, problematizador, del que muchos participamos, algunos con mas

in our hands, in our brains, in our eyes, a long, ongoing conversation that is already old, among ourselves, of each with him- or herself, with other architects and with other others—like a fluid that advances and maintains a fairly erratic trajectory, jumps unexpectedly, doubles back and describes very different trajectories; not just circles and spirals, but also random figures, slow and awkward, or at times extremely fast, vectorial like arrows. What is important, however, is not the (symbolic) geometry of the trajectories, but the fact that it is not the origin or the destination that matters; what matters is the act of flowing, the pleasure of the physical or mental journey, of being transported.

When we talk, things are consumed and other, new things appear: conversation is this act of advancing, leaving some subjects and starting others, describing trajectories, making journeys in the mind. There is an architecture like this, made up of "captures" (to cite Soriano, another sophist), instant mixtures, fixes, scraps, explosive mixtures—particularly of mixtures that always go unnoticed by the professionals of commentary (commentary being the opposite of conversation).

Citing conversation as the origin of a project brings to mind Rorty and his analogy of philosophy as conversation, a lot like the attachment to the problematizing, essayistic knowledge that many of us share—some more rigorously than others.

Iñaki Ábalos and Juan Herreros

But he is not alone: when he evokes this image, he does so as a sophist, a nominalist, an outsider, worldly, superficial, contingent. This way of acting and moving is typical of those who have no origin or destination, who do not need to work vertically, drawn taut between the sky and the centre of the earth like an infinite, abstract kebab on a skewer. They are steeped in lightness, in intense superficiality (it is in the skin that sensations, contact and exchange with the world take place)—the opposite of those who close their eyes and their mouths to see the truth revealed in their interior, given for once and for all.

Opening your eyes and your voice—"seeing with new eyes"—and, above all, becoming skin in full contact with the ground, completely flat, extensive, knowing the value of words, the persuasion of images, public and political, moving freely around the agora, talking, discussing, acknowledging no owner, proudly demonstrating unconcern for what does not draw us and desire for what amazes us. Is there such a thing as an architecture of conversation? It would be an architecture that sets out to be part of a dialogue, to join the forum and the debate, that speaks and expresses a vision of the world—or, to be more precise, of contemporary material culture. It is, so to speak, an architecture that has no goals, capital letters or prototypes to emulate: it is not the reflection of a Guiding Principle and it is unacquainted with universals (but nor does it have to contort itself in

relajo que otros. Pero no está solo: cuando invoca esta imagen lo hace en tanto que sofista, que nominalista, que hombre del exterior, mundano, superficial, contingente. Esta forma de actuar y moverse es la propia de quien carece de origen y destino, de quien no necesita trabajar en vertical, atado al cielo y al centro de la tierra como un pincho moruno abstracto e infinito, sino plenamente imbuido de ligereza, de intensa superficialidad (es en la piel donde se producen las sensaciones, el contacto, los intercambios con el mundo): es lo contrario de quien cierra los ojos y la boca para ver la verdad en su interior, revelada, dada de una vez para siempre.

Abrir los ojos y la voz -"mirar con nuevos ojos"- y sobre todo ser piel pegada al suelo, todo plano, extenso, sabedor del valor de las palabras, de la persuasión de las imágenes: público y político, campear por el ágora, hablar, discutir, no reconocer dueños, mostrar con orgullo indolencia por lo que no nos atrae y deseo cuando algo nos asombra. ¿Existe una arquitectura de la conversación?. Podría ser una arquitectura que quiere dialogar, salir al foro, al debate, que dice y expresa una visión del mundo o, para ser mas precisos, de la cultura material contemporánea. Es por así decirlo una arquitectura que no tiene meta, mayúsculas, prototipo que emular: no es el reflejo de ninguna Idea Rectora, no conoce los universales (y sin embargo no tiene por qué retorcerse expresando geométricamente angustia ni gritar forrándose de guiños semánticos representacionales). No representa: Es, tiene su propio estar, como si su especificidad técnica y topológica le diese alas, sabiduría y educación, y pudiese andar así por su cuenta, colocarse, mirar, decir: soy y estoy por mí misma; aunque no represento a nadie, no eludo mi sentido cívico. Si no respeto la tradición es porque me importa poco pero quizás si mirases mejor no me encontrarías tan indiferente; al menos no soy maleducada, dejo pasar delante a mis mayores, sé qué es lo que hago. Algo así. Pero, sobre todo, no tiene modelo final, no hay Tipo ni Cabaña ni esas cosas, su tiempo es plano, hecho de intensidades particulares.

No es nuevo esto: solo existe gótico ideal, catedral gótica ideal en la mente de Viollet, jamás en las de los maestros de Reims, Lyon, Amiens. Ellos conversaban, todo el pensamiento escolástico -urbano, comercial, de vuelta a la ciudad y al espacio cívico es una cultura del diálogo (el paso de los eremitas a las órdenes mendicantes, de la "fuga mundi" a las "disputatio" escolásticas). No hay trayecto lineal: hay itinerancia, vagabundeo de las ideas, ida y vuelta, reelaboración, captura, polarizaciones... También Vandelvira establece un diálogo maravilloso con la técnica, el lenguaje, las circunstancias locales, la vida coetánea andaluza. La catedral de Jaén, ese palacio civil vuelto del revés, esa Lonja atea, gótica y humanista a la vez, es una arquitectura que habla con los arquitectos -con Siloé- y con las ciudades, que administra sus herencias abriendo nuevas perspectivas.

Quien conversa es contextualista, es sofista (Sota y el Oiza pre M-30) pero no en un sentido pequeño, geométrico, material o proporcional, sino puro: actúa reaccionando frente a los estímulos de un contexto que es su tiempo en un sentido amplio. Un contextualista no esta en medio gozosamente lleno de contexto, esta tangente, toca y se retira; es escéptico, tiene que alejarse porque quiere ver globalmente, operar

geometric expressions of anguish or scream out with a battery of obscure semantic representational references). It does not represent; it is. It has its own being, as though its technical and topological specificity gives it wings, wisdom and education, and it can stand on its own, adopt a stance, look, and say, I exist and I am here in my own right; I do not represent anyone, but I do not shirk my civic commitment. If I do not respect tradition, it is because I care little for it, but perhaps if you looked more closely, you would not find me so indifferent. At least I am not ill mannered; I give way to my elders, I know what I am doing. Something along those lines. But, most of all, it has no ultimate model; there is no Type or Hut or any of those things. Its time is flat, comprised of particular intensities.

This is nothing new. The Gothic ideal and the ideal Gothic cathedral exist only in the mind of Viollet-le-Duc, never in those of the masters of Rheims, Lyon or Amiens. They conversed; all scholastic thinking—urban, commercial, back to the city and civic space—is a culture of dialogue (the shift from hermits to mendicant orders, from *fuga mundi* to the scholastic *disputatio*). There is no linear path; there is itinerancy, a wandering of ideas, there and back again, reworking, capture and polarizations. De Vandelvira also created a marvellous dialogue with technology, language, local circumstance and Andalusian life. Jaén cathedral, that civic palace turned inside out, that

Iñaki Ábalos and Juan Herreros

hall that is at once humanist, Gothic and atheist, is an architecture that speaks with architects—with De Siloé— and with cities, that manages its legacies by creating new perspectives.

To converse is to be a contextualist, a sophist (De la Sota, and Sáenz de Oiza before the M-30), not in a small, geometric, material or proportional way, but purely: it is to act by reacting to the stimuli of a context that is one's time, in the broadest sense. Contextualists do not stand cheerfully in the middle, set roundly in context; they are tangent, they connect and withdraw; they are skeptical; they have to step back because they want to see the big picture, act holistically and avoid excessive pawing. They go in and out.

Their minds operate globally. They can interrupt the conversation to take it to a distant point and describe a path that, finally, casts light unexpectedly on the original subject. The rhetorical mind wanders, forms clouds and stirs things up. All projects are contained in this wandering that only catalyzes or liquefies when it comes across precise stimuli, perhaps in unforeseeable directions. When does a cloud produce precipitation? When it collides with another, when there is friction. This is what conversation is: battering ideas by running them up against other ideas, taking them to the unforeseeable. Conversation moves things toward collision. But none of this means anything without the

holísticamente, evitar el manoseo. Entra y sale.

Su mente opera globalmente. Puede cortar la conversación para llevarla a un punto lejano y describir un trayecto que se atraviesa y finalmente ilumina por sorpresa el tema original. La mente retórica vagabundea, hace nubes, se remueve. Todos los proyectos estan en ese vagabundear que solo se cataliza, se licúa, ante estímulos precisos, quizá en direcciones imprevisibles. ¿Como se precipita una nube?: chocando con otra, entrando en fricción. Eso es lo que es la conversación: abollar las ideas cruzándolas con otras, llevándolas a lo imprevisible. La conversación empuja hacia el choque. Pero nada de esto se entiende si no se defiende la novedad, la importancia de lo nuevo por sí mismo.

Preferir lo nuevo como reacción, precisamente porque falta aquí y ahora, todo tan prudente y despacio, con tanto cuidado y modestia (falsa): "aportemos nuestro granito de arena", "un eslabón mas", "todo conduce siempre a lo mismo", "en la historia esta la respuesta..."

Sí sí, ya lo sabemos, pero no queremos dar respuestas, sólo queremos hacer preguntas mas astutas. Estamos ligados a Vandelvira, pero

Edificio administrativo para el Ministerio del Interior. Madrid. Arquitectos: Ábalos y Herreros. Fotografía: Manolo Laguillo

también a Shin-ju-Ku, a Freud, y a Schömberg, y al Banco de Bilbao, y a toda la música pop, y a Carver y a tantos tiempos, cosas, personas, lugares que si de este dejarse atravesar solo sale un poquito mas de lo mismo -justo lo que no pasa con quienes nos atraviesan- daría asco, un cacho de asco importante, un buen pedazo de aburrimiento.

Lyotard dice "recuerden que el techné griego es a un tiempo arte y lo que llamamos tecnología. Recuerden también que la tecnología siempre implica nueva tecnología". Tecnología siempre implica nueva tecnología. No se trata de una sensación

7

defence of novelty, the importance of the new in itself.

Preferring the new as a reaction, precisely because it's missing here and now; everything is so cautious and slow, so careful and (falsely) modest: "let's all do our part," "one more link in the chain," "everything always leads to the same result," "history has all the answers…"

Yes, yes, we know; but we're not looking to give answers. We just want to ask cleverer questions. We are linked with Vandelvira, but also with Shinjuku, Freud and Schönberg, with Oiza's Bank of Bilbao, pop music as a whole, Carver and so many times, people and places that if this letting oneself be invaded only produced a little more of the same—precisely what doesn't happen to those who invade us—it would be sickening, big-time sickening, mind-numbingly boring.

Lyotard says: "Remember that the Greek's *techné* is at once art and what we call technology. Remember, too, that technology always means new technology." Technology always means new technology. This is not an irrational sensation; the question of novelty is always linked to the way we operate, to the material culture of an age (we might say "modern," the cynical mantra of those who call themselves modern yet hate modes). Possessing technique, coming into possession of technique, means embracing the possibility of using its two products: tools and weapons.

Iñaki Ábalos and Juan Herreros

It means constructing a machine —such as this mediatic *CIRCO*— that is capable of undoing the fiction that what already exists is Everything, and arming us with tools to make the Other. Breaking and making at the same time. This is the new and the drive toward it. This is why our interest in material culture has always been to say: it is not true that only this can be done here. It might have been, once, but it is not now, not for us. Our time is another, and everything, from the way we operate to the tools, the feel and the look, can all be different, and it is best that it should be. Let's look here: it's better and more attractive, it's different, something new and exciting might even come of it. Don't make me lay more bricks, please! I know those thick walls, solid, well built and stable forever; I don't want them.

I like what is there but might slip away if you don't see it. It is mine; I enjoy it, and I like it all the more. It is a question of context. With what do I operate? With what there is, with what is "out there." I do not judge it, I do not know if it is good or bad; I wouldn't know that of anything or anyone. It is there and it is mine, it may be exciting, it makes things light and easy, it is mobile and elusive, it dialogues, it interests me, it reflects me. But, more than anything, it is my nature, I belong to it, I move in it, literally and figuratively. Clouds and their reflection in the photograph by Laguillo express it best of all.

irracional, la cuestión de la novedad esta ligada a nuestro modo de operar, a la cultura material de una época (podría hablarse de la palabra moderno, de la cínica cantinela de quienes dicen ser modernos y odian la moda). Poseer la técnica, entrar en posesión de la técnica es abrir la posibilidad de usar sus dos productos: las herramientas y las armas; es construir una máquina -p.ej. este Circo mediático- capaz de deshacer la ficción de que lo ya dado es Todo y tener en la mano los útiles para hacer lo Otro. Romper y fabricar a la vez. Eso es lo nuevo y el impulso hacia él. Por eso nuestro interés por la cultura material ha sido decir: no es verdad que aquí solo pueda hacerse esto. Quizás lo fue pero ahora no, no para nosotros, nuestro tiempo es otro y todo, desde la forma en que operamos, a los utensilios, el tacto o la mirada, todo puede ser distinto y es mejor que lo sea. Miremos aquí, es mejor, mas atractivo, distinto, incluso es posible que salga algo nuevo y que emocione; no me haga poner mas ladrillos por favor, ya sé lo que son sus paredes, gordas, bien hechas, robustas, para siempre, bien fundadas: no las quiero.

Me gusta lo que esta ahí y puede escaparse si no lo ves, es mío, disfruto y me gusta más. Es una cuestión contextual. ¿Con qué opero?. Con lo que hay, con lo que esta ahí "afuera". No lo juzgo, no sé si es bueno o malo, no lo sabría de nada ni de nadie. Esta ahí, es mío, puede ser emocionante, hace las cosas fáciles y ligeras, es móvil y escurridizo, dialoga, me interesa, me refleja. Pero mas que nada es mi naturaleza, pertenezco a ella, me muevo en ella, en un sentido literal y figurado. Las nubes y su reflejo en la fotografía de Laguillo lo expresan mejor que nada.

Then there is the ordinary, the "as is": partaking in a material wisdom that is the heritage of our age (the child with a remote control). It is realizing that entering into this popular culture is less paternalistic than the figurative attitude of Pop (Venturi's "Let's give people adverts, history and flowers; that's what they want"), that there is a way of living with the remote control that is not in your face, that does not thematize the phenomenon, but uses it (like the child). Charles Eames is a reference: another converser, with another body of work in full contact with the ground.

Doing things with fewer things is not nostalgia for Mies; it means knowing that if things get tough, you are on the wrong path. It means not solving problems or shaking them off and joining another conversation when a hopeless someone or other interferes in ours.

This brings us to the subject of space, which someone addressed in a previous *CIRCO*. From the point of view of the converser, this phenomenological, existential space is old and loaded; it just doesn't cut the mustard. It's odd to talk about essences if you're under forty, and you'd be embarrassed if your old friends overheard you. We wouldn't get anywhere if we stuck with Heidegger and an essential space against forgetting. The phenomenological space leads to contemplation, self-absorption: it is an inward-looking gaze that seeks to bind us to the place by invading us from somewhere

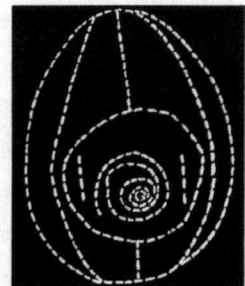
Huevo dogón

Además, esta la vulgaridad: el "tal cual", participar de una sabiduría material que es patrimonio de nuestra época (el niño manejando mandos a distancia). Entender que entrar en esta cultura popular es menos paternalista que la actitud figurativa del pop, -"demos anuncios, historia y flores a la gente, es lo que quieren" (Venturi)-, que existe una forma de habitar en el mando a distancia que no es gritona, que no tematiza el fenómeno sino que lo usa (como el niño). Charles Eames es una referencia, otro conversador, otro trabajo hecho pegado al suelo.

Hacer las cosas con menos cosas no es nostalgia de Mies, es saber que siempre cuando las cosas se ponen difíciles el camino estaba equivocado. No resolver problemas, quitárselos de encima, entrar en otra conversación cuando hay un torpe en la que estamos.

Así se llega al tema del espacio que alguien ya ha tratado en un Circo anterior. Desde la perspectiva del conversador ese espacio existencial, fenomenológico, es antiguo, cargado de intención, no pasa, queda mal: hablar de esencias con menos de 40 años es

9

Iñaki Ábalos and Juan Herreros

back in time. It is a hermeneutic, centred gaze, a nostalgia for the thickness and depth of the works of the past (a thickness and a depth that are added by that filter called culture: today, Warhol is already perceived with this thickness).

We have to defend—as it has so few allies—a more outward-looking attitude that slides over the surface without binding itself either to the place or to the past, that sees with cunning—no innocence, please!—and speed, that intensifies the relation that can be established with the world and avoids stopping to contemplate, instead wandering over things with no particular affection or rejection.

The space that is the primordial stuff of this gaze of the skin, this gaze of surfaces, porous and swift, is quantitative space, the square metre as precisely that—the introduction of m² as a value in our society. Banal space. Wresting emotion from ordinary physical space, not negotiating with morality, refusing to enter into categories of value.

It is more judicious to recognize the existence of the spirit of the bricklayer, the need for the wall; to recognize that there is a world that needs refuge, that looks back, that is just off mom and dad's room, and another world that flows, that needs air and lightness, if only because it is the one hole with light, the light of surprise, or something different in itself. It has no walls or stable forms, it's difficult for an architect to know what

extraño, daría vergüenza que te oyeran tus viejos amigos. No avanzaríamos en ninguna dirección si siguiéramos con Heidegger y un espacio esencial en contra del olvido. El espacio fenomenológico obliga a la contemplación, el ensimismamiento: es una mirada hacia dentro que quiere atarnos al lugar atravesándonos hacia atrás en el tiempo. Es una mirada centrada, hermenéutica, una nostalgia del espesor, de la profundidad de las obras del pasado (un espesor y una profundidad añadidos a posteriori por ese filtro que es la cultura: ya hoy Warhol es percibido con ese espesor).

Hay que defender -pues apenas tiene aliados- una actitud mas exterior que se desliza por la superficie y no se ata ni al lugar ni al pasado: que ve con malicia -nada de inocencia por favor- y rapidez, que intensifica la relación que puede establecerse con el mundo eludiendo pararse a contemplar, vagabundeando sobre las cosas sin especial afecto o rechazo.

El espacio que es materia primordial de esa mirada con la piel, de superficie, porosa y rápida es el espacio cuantitativo, el metro cuadrado como tal, esa instauración del m2 como valor en nuestra sociedad. El espacio banal. Arrancarle emoción al medio físico vulgar, no negociar con la moral, negarse a entrar en categorías de valor.

Es mas certero saber que existe el espíritu enladrillador, la necesidad de la pared, saber que existe un mundo que necesita el refugio, que mira para atrás, que se alimenta del cuarto de papá y mamá, y un mundo que fluye, que necesita aire y ligereza aunque solo sea porque es el único agujero con luz, la luz de la

material it is made of (is it material?) and the models come from other disciplines. It is the Thunderbird of *Thelma and Louise* versus Freud's office. It is working with desire, owning that desire by opposing a forward-moving conversation to a confession from the past. But desire has no rooms; it flees or it comes toward us like the letters in the *Sign o' the Times* video; you have to operate with things and images unrelated to representation, and our whole education is different.

All we know is that it's best to stay on the edge, in the position of the cynic, the sophist, the Machiavellian, the rhetorician, the pragmatist or the cosmopolitan; to make things reproduce this position, to remain tangent and involved, but set to make a move. To make them resemble the form in which they are conceived, like this article, like a mixture of subjects that intersect and prowl around each other. In this way, ultimately we would be able to speak to things. In fact, we all do it constantly—we prick up our ears and, suddenly, one day we start to understand their language, and we discover that they talk to us, just like Francis the mule, and tell us what they want to be like. But that's another issue. We end on this note with a quote from a telltale schizophrenic dream:

"There is a desert. Again, it wouldn't make any sense to say that I am *in* the desert. It's a panoramic view of the desert, and it is not a tragic or uninhabited desert. It's only a desert because of its ochre colour and

Iñaki Ábalos and Juan Herreros

its blazing, shadowless sun. There is a teeming crowd in it, a swarm of bees, a rumble of soccer players or a group of Tuareg. I am on the edge of the crowd, at the periphery; but I belong to it. I am attached to it by one of my extremities, a hand or a foot. I know that the periphery is the only place I can be, that I would die if I let myself be drawn into the centre of the fray, but just as certainly if I let go of the crowd. This is not an easy position to stay in; it is even very difficult to hold, for these beings are in constant motion and their movements are unpredictable and follow no rhythm. They swirl, go north, then suddenly east; none of the individuals in the crowd remains in the same place in relation to the others. So I, too, am in perpetual motion; all this demands a high level of tension, but it gives me a feeling of violent, almost vertiginous, happiness."

periferia; pero pertenezco a ella, estoy unida a ella por una extremidad de mi cuerpo, una mano o un pie. Sé que esta periferia es el único lugar posible para mi, moriría si me dejara arrastrar al centro de la melé. Pero seguramente me sucedería lo mismo si abandonara. Mi posición no es fácil de conservar, incluso diría que es muy dificil de mantener, porque esos seres se mueven sin parar, sus movimientos son imprevisibles y no responden a ningún ritmo. Unas veces se arremolinan, otras van hacia el norte y luego, bruscamente, hacia el este, sin que ninguno de los individuos que componen la multitud mantenga la misma posición con relación a los demás. Así pues, también yo estoy en perpetuo movimiento, y eso exige una gran tensión, pero a la vez me proporciona un sentimiento de felicidad violento, casi vertiginoso".

Iñaki Abalos, Juan Herreros.
Noviembre 1.993

Papel ecológico sin ácidos.

Images: Book burning in Berlin, 1933 / Administrative building for the Ministry of the Interior, Madrid. Architects: Ábalos&Herreros. Photograph: Manolo Laguillo / Dogon egg

Out of the Box: Ábalos&Herreros
Giovanna Borasi

The Ábalos&Herreros archive was donated to the CCA by the architects Iñaki Ábalos and Juan Herreros in 2012. The archive, which is comprised of over 150 projects dating from 1986 to 2006, is mainly formed by sketches, drawings in both print and digital form, collages, related textual documents, slides and models. As always, an architectural archive is a fundamental repository of the architects' ideas, a crucial instrument for revealing their way of thinking and their design process. In the case of Ábalos&Herreros specifically, the archive holdings vividly illustrate their professional work—built projects as well as unrealized ideas for competitions—along with their research, writing, curating and teaching. What is not present in the archive also hints at their way of working: for example the absence of study models shows that Ábalos&Herreros did not privilege this medium, in their opinion time-consuming and of little help in their thinking process, and favoured collages instead.

Iñaki Ábalos and Juan Herreros established their office in Madrid in 1984, working together until 2008. Each initiated separate activities in 2009. In Madrid in the 1980s and 1990s, a period of transformation following the end of the Franco regime, architects were still valued for their technical ability and for their capacity to redefine the built environment. In this context, Ábalos&Herreros were remarkable for their different response to these assumptions: they deliberately established a permanent coexistence of theoretical research and professional work. This activity overlapped with their teaching at ETSAM (Escuela Técnica Superior de Arquitectura de Madrid), as well as with their publications and curatorial work.

Many ideas were developed in more than twenty years of the office. Ábalos&Herreros's way of working was based on conversation: conversation between the architects themselves, with collaborators in the office, with artists involved in their projects and with other architects through their teaching and writing. "Is there such a thing as an architecture of conversation?" Ábalos&Herreros ask in their text entitled "A Conversation," published in *CIRCO* 9 (1993). It is as if their architecture could be understood as the direct result of conversation between them and with past and contemporary architects; but most importantly it is as if architecture could be the tool with which and the field in which to express and debate ideas in relation to contemporary culture.

The many essays by Ábalos&Herreros on the work of other architects are then a facet of this approach and clearly explain and reconstruct their way of thinking. In their practice the project is developed through research, which implies finding the right tools, appropriating past experiences and defining new methods. This approach explains Ábalos&Herreros's interest in drawing from existing systems and arriving at a built form through minimal effort.

"At first we wanted to work on a very technical understanding of our discipline. So our first texts were mainly about technical issues, researched in a very rigorous way. But then we discovered the possibilities of working with the material we had at hand, offered by industry and commerce. Not necessarily to invent new systems but rather to manipulate existing technical, construction, spatial and commercial systems." This is how Ábalos&Herreros explained the initial stage of their work in an interview with Hans Ulrich Obrist (*2G*, no. 22), who met them following Cedric Price's strong recommendation. Price was fascinated by their work, and was particularly struck by their recycling plant in Valdemingómez, Madrid, which in his opinion was designed with "fresh ideas and appropriate materials." For Price, in this project "there's a sense of modesty linked to economy, linked to the process of real economy that shows a pride and delight in deciding on real priorities... It is a model of how you should handle consumer society before waste occurs. It's wonderful because it's a model for how society should approach the problem of recycling without being pompous" (2G, no. 22). In Price's view, Ábalos & Hererros had the capacity to embrace incompleteness and uncertainty, as they demonstrated in the 2000 exhibition *Potteries Thinkbelt (PTb), 1964–66: caducidad, educación y energía,* designed by Ábalos & Herreros and curated by Juan Herreros: "I thought the show was very good when it concentrated on the incompleteness of my own work seen as a useful prediction of what might happen in the future."

Many architects and critics have observed, studied and commented on the work of Ábalos & Herreros while the firm was active, but these readings were mainly based on their built work and their ongoing research activities. The arrival of the archive at the CCA presents a new opportunity for observation and discovery based on materials related to process rather than to the final built projects. The CCA acquired the Ábalos & Herreros archive along with several other archives that relate to contemporary architecture practice, most recently the archives of Foreign Office Architects (FOA), known as AP171 according to the CCA's archival structure, and of Álvaro Siza, or AP178. The CCA is interested in Ábalos & Herreros's work and therefore in their archive for many reasons, including their anticipatory commitment to environmental issues; the relationship they established with technology without fetishizing it; their interpretation of the notion of landscape; their idea of an economy of means; their sophisticated pragmatism; their connection of their work to the history of architecture; and of course the way they ran their practice, in which teaching, writing, curating and design were all facets of the same larger project.

The intention of the CCA is to activate these recent acquisitions upon their arrival by immediately initiating a process of research and investigation, foreseeing a unique opportunity to exhibit this unseen material to the public while taking an active part in the contemporary debate on architecture. This is a broader strategy toward archival holdings entitled Out of the Box, in which the CCA actively exposes archival material to a process of research and discovery while the archive is still being organized and catalogued. Generally, the institutional procedures concerning collection materials are linear: acquisition, followed by cataloguing, research, exhibition and publication. In the Out of the Box strategy, the CCA proposes to develop all these activities in parallel: acquisition, research and exhibition occur simultaneously. This temporal shift produces a series of constructive and unexpected changes in the activities themselves: research is present throughout, and in particular the exhibition becomes a research tool that presents provisional results. The CCA initiated this approach to archiving and research with the 2003 exhibition *out of the box: price rossi stirling + matta-clark*, curated by Mirko Zardini with Mark Wigley, Marco

De Michelis, Anthony Vidler and Philip Ursprung as co-curators respectively of the four sections on each architect.

To continue and develop this approach with the Ábalos&Herreros archive, the CCA conceived a new program that strengthens the connection between archival material, research and public presentation of the collection. The program consists of a research residency, for which individual scholars and collectives are invited to study and interpret the work in the CCA archives. The recipients are selected in accordance with their connection to the archive's content and the relevance of their experience and expertise. The selection of these specific researchers and curators was also driven by a clear view of where their interests, both intellectually and formally, reside and by the belief that these interests would resonate with what the CCA intended to reveal at the moment of opening of the archive of Ábalos&Herreros's work.

In this case, the selected researchers and curators—Kersten Geers and David Van Severen of OFFICE Kersten Geers David Van Severen (Brussels), Juan José Castellón González from ETH Zurich and Florian Idenburg and Jing Liu of SO – IL (New York)—were invited for residencies of two weeks between October and November 2014, designed as focused immersions in the Ábalos&Herreros archive. Each group determined a precise line of investigation and articulated a way of reading the archive and the architects' work. They all dug in the archive, each one with a precise set of questions in mind. Kersten Geers and David Van Severen, who studied under Ábalos&Herreros in Madrid, investigate the architects' fascination with an industrial approach to architecture. Juan José Castellón González, who worked with Ábalos& Herreros between 2003 and 2007, is interested in their capacity to construct a hybrid materiality while avoiding any manifestation of the building technology as a language. Florian Idenburg and Jing Liu, who share many academic endeavors with Iñaki Ábalos and Juan Herreros, are interested in their approach to inhabiting an urban or rural site and their visions for new landscapes. These critical arguments, paths of investigation and opposing points of view generated a series of seminars and discussions and ultimately three Out of the Box exhibitions held in the CCA's Octagonal Gallery between March and September 2015. Ideas, writings and discussions developed during the program are collected in this publication. The strong connection between practice, writing and teaching is made evident in different ways in all three readings: the idea of an economy of means and repetition of solutions appears in Geers and Van Severen's *Industrial Architecture* and in Castellón's *Jai Tech*, while a reading of the context and of Ábalos&Herreros's skill at imagining new programmatic strategies and new landscapes is analyzed by Castellón, and by Idenburg and Liu in *Landscapes of the Hyperreal*.

This program applied to architects who are still active in the field allows for a different approach to archival research in the field of the history of architecture: Iñaki Ábalos and Juan Herreros themselves, as subjects of study, also play an active role as respondents to the different proposed readings and research, and their voices are present in annotations and reactions in the book. This enhances the debate, but it also creates an immediate oral history.

Through this research program and the resulting series of exhibitions, the CCA creates a unique opportunity to develop a critical discourse concerning contemporary archives and architectural practices. The project is also an attempt to reintroduce theoretical research and critical thinking into the practice of architecture. While taking an active part in contemporary debates, the CCA supports the emergence of new voices in the field and new methods of scholarly research. The idea of introducing from the beginning multiple and simultaneous lines of investigation will initiate different forms of research and diverse readings of the architects' work while challenging the idea of monographic work, understood as the work of a single researcher on a single subject. The conversations, which Ábalos&Herreros established in their office and with colleagues and other architects whose work interested them, are now taking a new form, gaining new voices and continuing through their archive. It is also important to acknowledge an additional intentionality of the project: as no research is innocent, the specific readings by Kersten Geers and David Van Severen, by Juan José Castellón González, and by Florian Idenburg and Jing Liu say just as much about the work and the interests of this new generation of architects as they do about the work of Ábalos&Herreros. For the researchers, this immersion in the vaults was like looking in a mirror.

In November 2014, Stefano Graziani was invited to interpret the archive of Ábalos&Herreros in photographs. The series he produced consists of views of archival documents and objects, and the photographs are now themselves part of the CCA collection.

Proofs of Relevance
Stefano Graziani

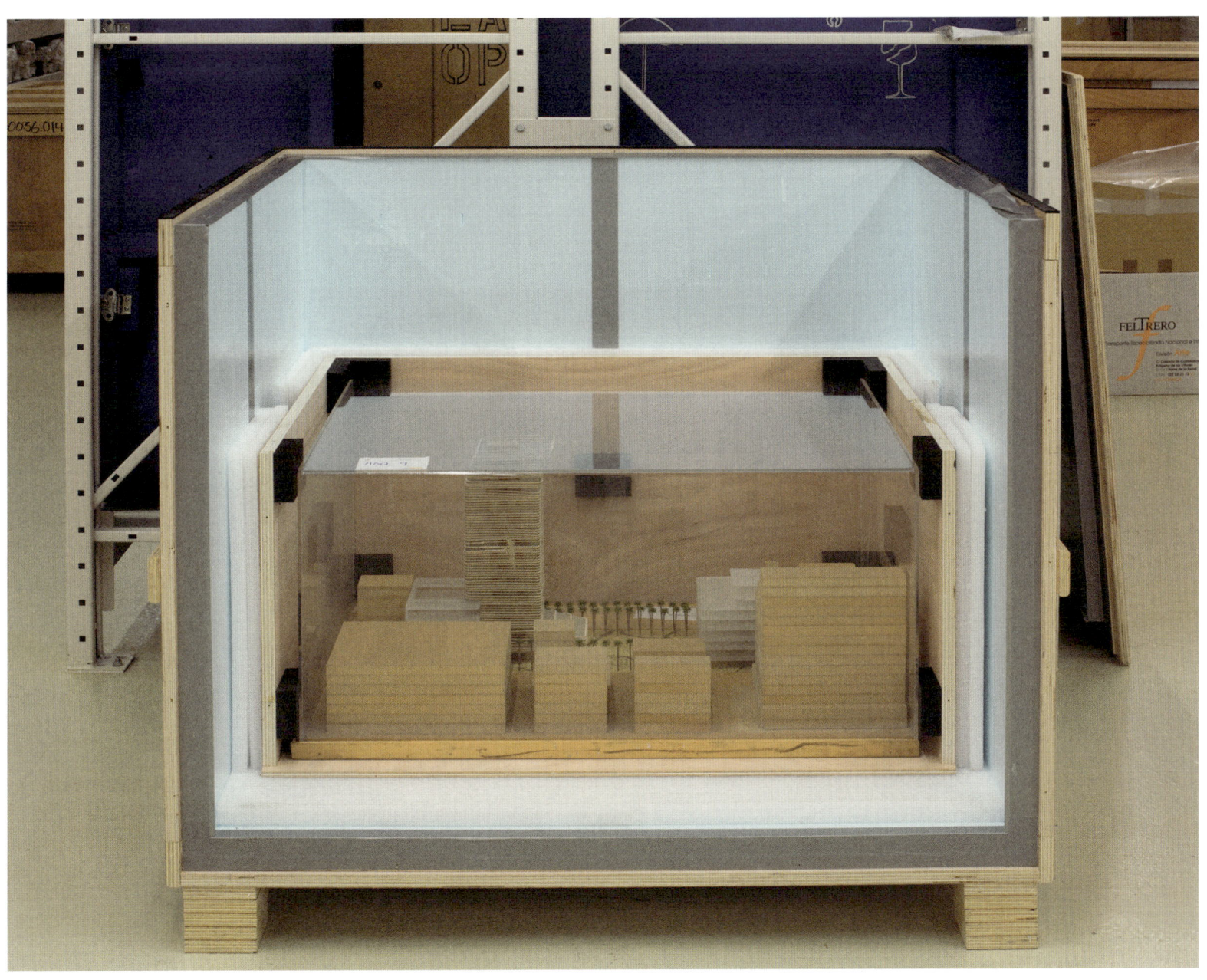

Stefano Graziani

Stefano Graziani

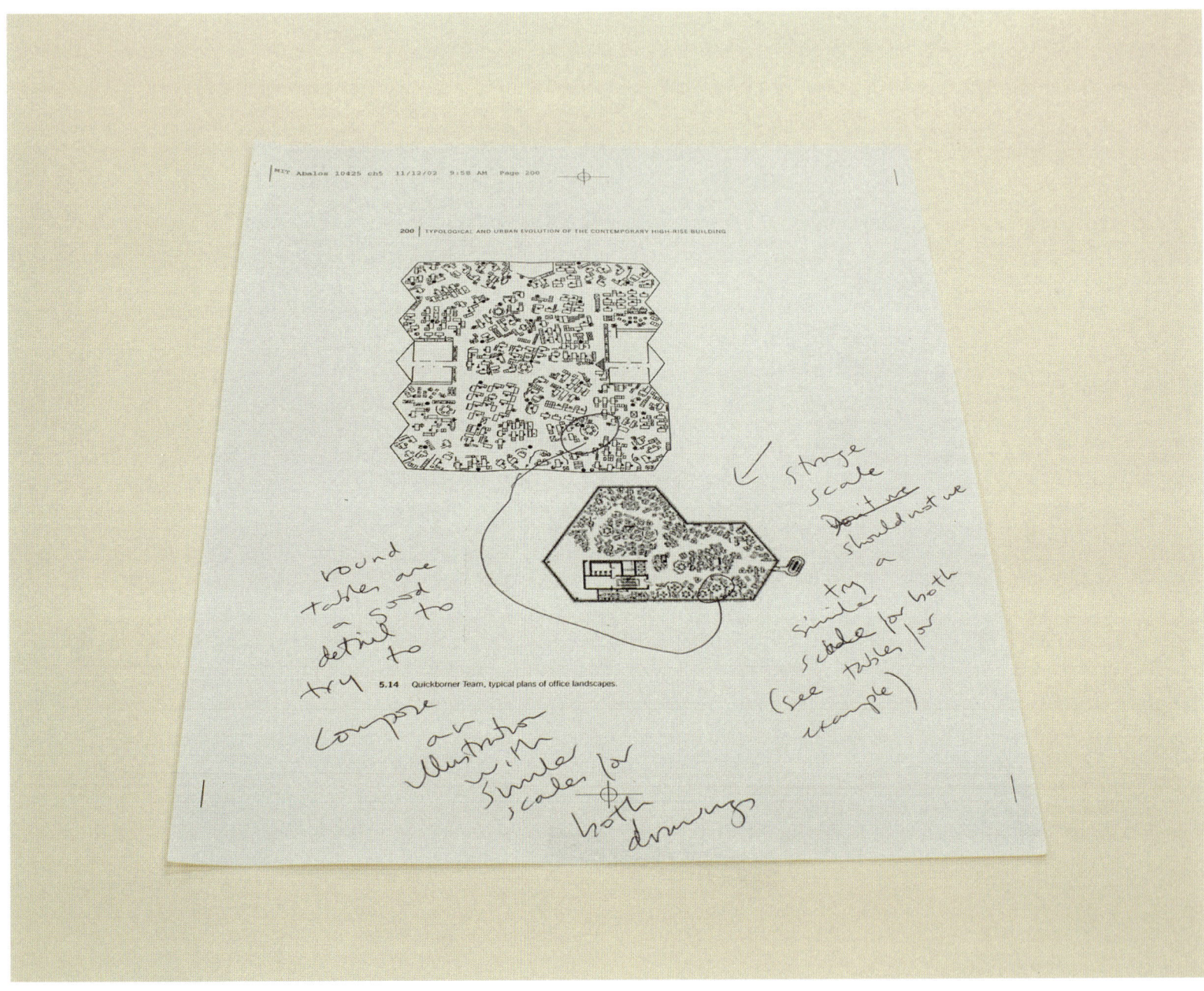

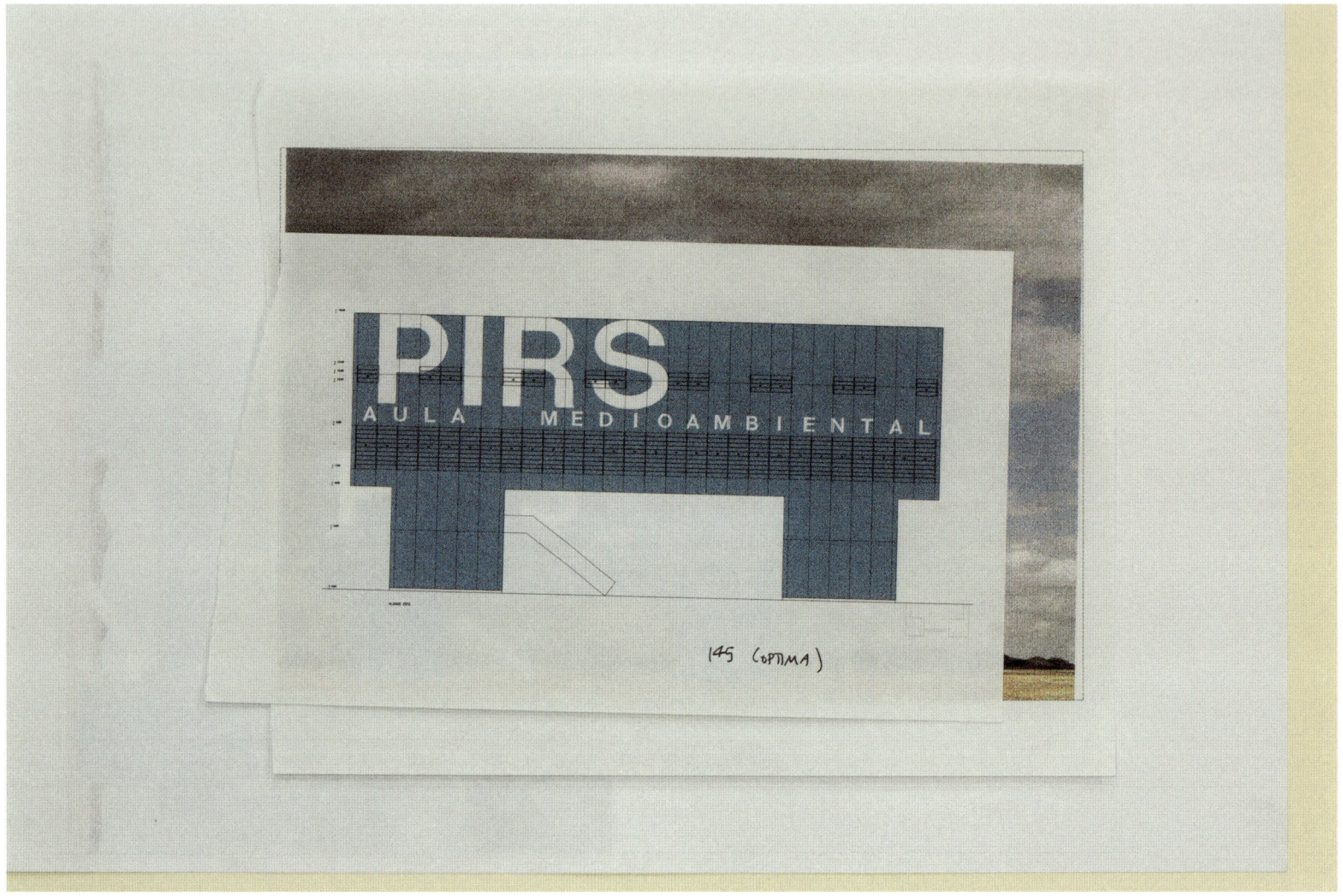

Stefano Graziani

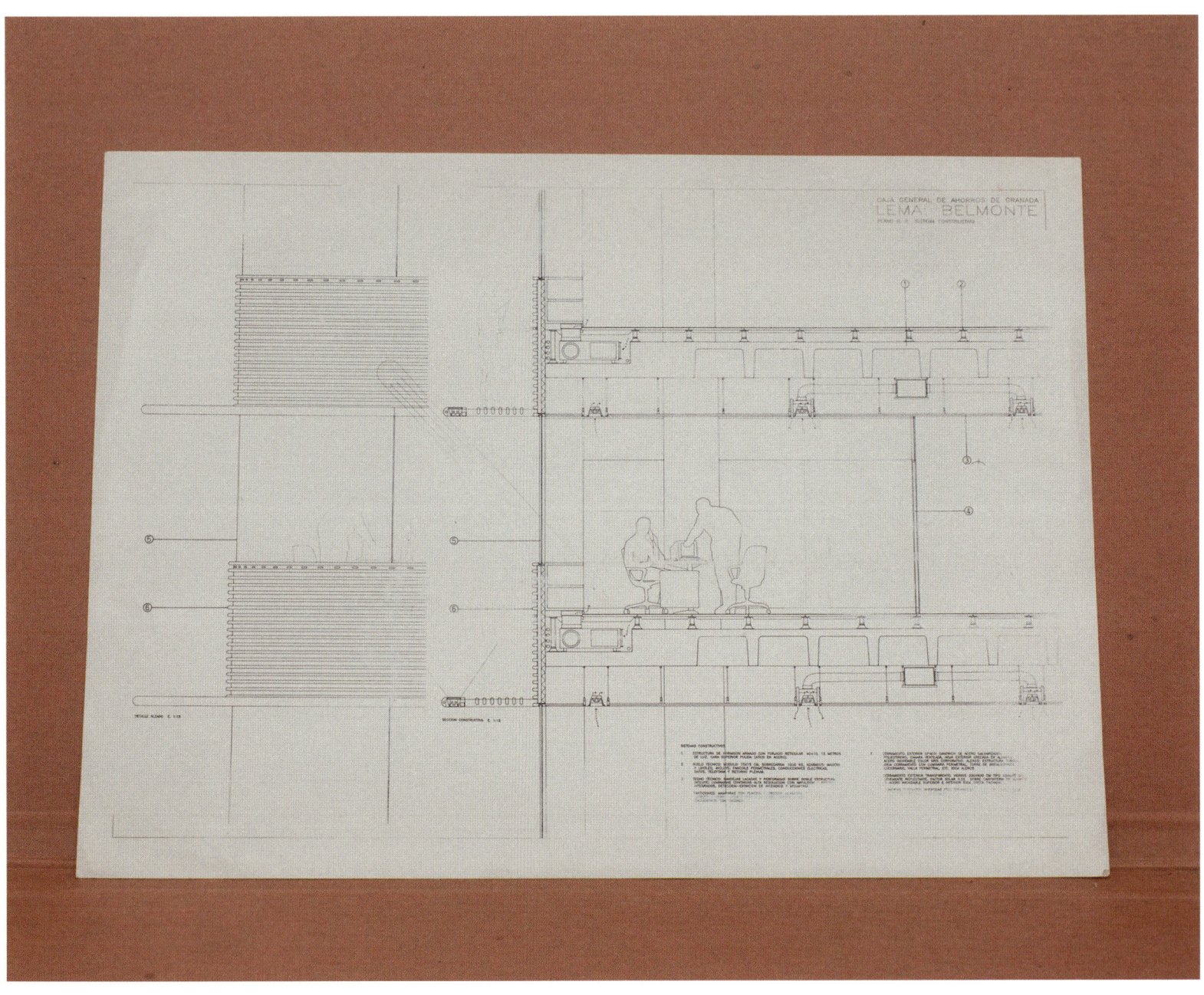

Stefano Graziani

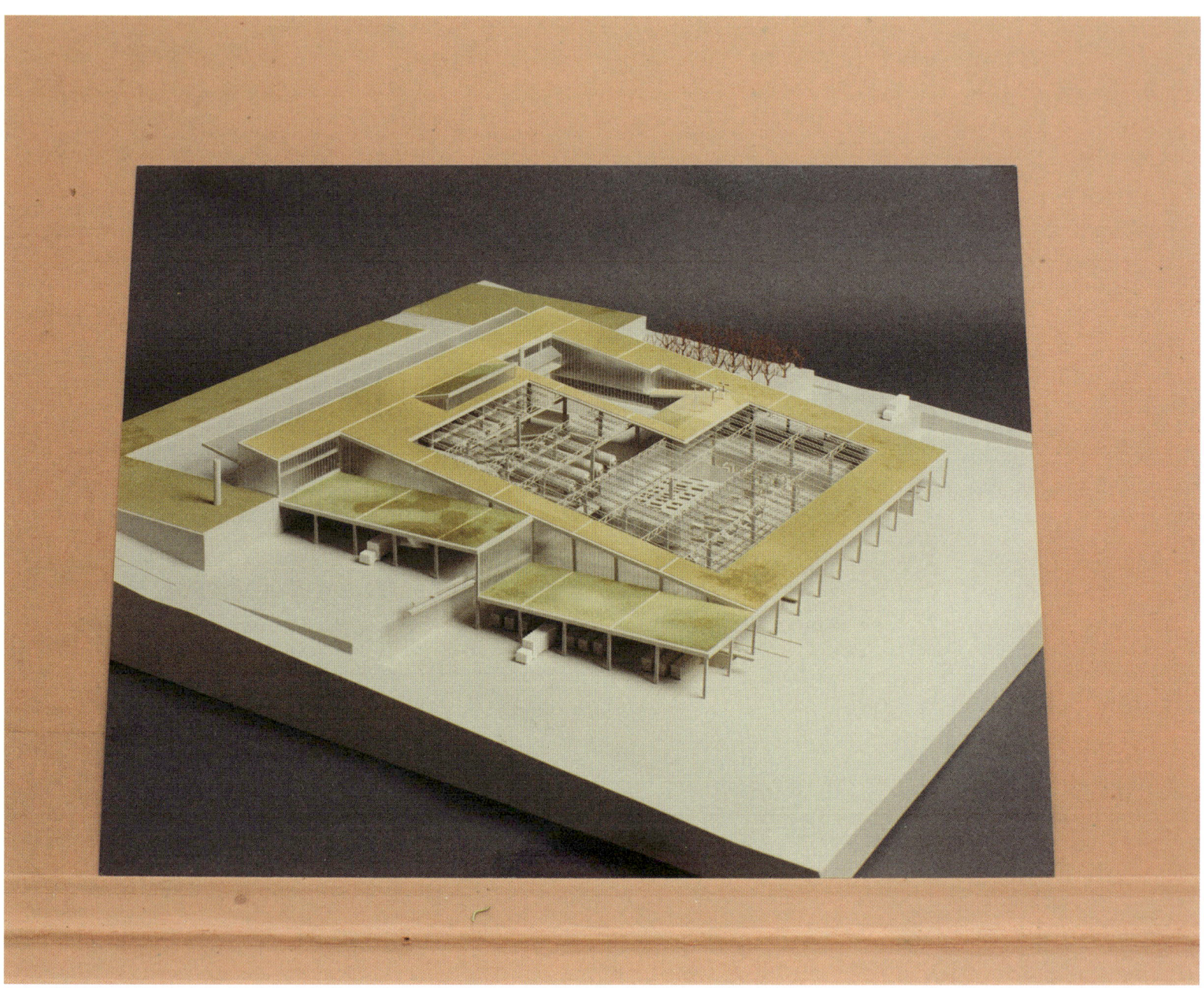

Stefano Graziani

p. 29. View of a model of the Woermann Plaza and Tower, Las Palmas de Gran Canaria, 2001–2005 (AP164.S1.2001.D7). Digital print, 20 × 24.9 cm. PH2015:0002:025

p. 30. View of a photograph of a model of Usera library, Madrid, 1995–2003 (AP164.S1.1995.D1). Digital print, 20 × 24.9 cm. PH2015:0002:010

p. 31. View of a model of one of the four environmental mixed-use towers in the Salburua wetlands, Vitoria-Gasteiz, 2002–2006 (AP164.S1.2002.D2). Digital print, 20 × 24.9 cm. PH2015:0002:043

p. 32. View of a computer screen showing a reference image for Einsteinet, office building and showroom, Hamburg, 2000 (AP164.S1.2000.D7). Digital print, 20 × 24.9 cm. PH2015:0002:022

p. 33. View of a collage for the industrialized housing prototypes: AH-Gia Houses, 1993–1996 (AP164.S1.1993.D11). Digital print, 20 × 24.9 cm. PH2015:0002:005

p. 34. View of a photograph of a model of the New Museum of Contemporary Art, New York, 2003 (AP164.S1.2003.D1). Digital print, 20 × 24.9 cm. PH2015:0002:012

p. 35. View of a model of one of the four environmental mixed-use towers in the Salburua wetlands, Vitoria-Gasteiz, 2002–2006 (AP164.S1.2002.D2). Digital print, 20 × 24.9 cm. PH2015:0002:044

p. 36. View of an annotated page of the manuscript "Tower and Office: From Modernist Theory to Contemporary Practice" by Iñaki Ábalos and Juan Herreros, 2002. Digital print, 20 × 24.9 cm. PH2015:0002:020

p. 37. View of a collage for the industrialized housing prototypes: AH-Gia Houses, 1993–1996 (AP164.S1.1993.D11). Digital print, 20 × 24.9 cm. PH2015:0002:003

p. 38. View of a collage for the industrialized housing prototypes: AH-Gia Houses, 1993–1996 (AP164.S1.1993.D11). Digital print, 20 × 24.9 cm. PH2015:0002:002

p. 39. View of a model of one of the four environmental mixed-use towers in the Salburua wetlands, Vitoria-Gasteiz, 2002–2006 (AP164.S1.2002.D2). Digital print, 20 × 24.9 cm. PH2015:0002:041

p. 40. View of a photomontage showing the environmental education centre and offices, Arico, Tenerife, 1998–2001 (AP164.S1.1998.D1). Digital print, 20 × 29.9 cm. PH2015:0002:045

p. 41. View of a photomontage showing the environmental education centre and offices, Arico, Tenerife, 1998–2001 (AP164.S1.1998.D1). Digital print, 20 × 29.9 cm. PH2015:0002:046

p. 42. View of a drawing showing a section of the head office for the Savings Bank of Granada, 1992 (AP164.S1.1992.D4). Digital print, 20 × 24.9 cm. PH2015:0002:013

p. 43. View of a model of one of the four environmental mixed-use towers in the Salburua wetlands, Vitoria-Gasteiz, 2002–2006 (AP164.S1.2002.D2). Digital print, 20 × 24.9 cm. PH2015:0002:040

p. 44. View of a computer screen showing a digital rendering for the EPFL learning centre, Lausanne, 2004 (AP164.S1.2004.D9). Digital print, 20 × 24.9 cm. PH2015:0002:018

p. 45. View of a collage for the industrialized housing prototypes: AH-Gia Houses, 1993–1996 (AP164.S1.1993.D11). Digital print, 20 × 24.9 cm. PH2015:0002:006

p. 46. View of a photograph of a model of the recycling plant for urban waste, Valdemingómez, Madrid, 1996–1999 (AP164.S1.1996.D4). Digital print, 20 × 24.9 cm. PH2015:0002:028

p. 47. View of a reference photograph showing the steel system of a building under construction. Digital print, 20 × 24.9 cm. PH2015:0002:042

p. 48. View of a poster showing a photomontage for the New Museum of Contemporary Art, New York, 2003 (AP164.S1.2003.D1). Digital print, 20 × 24.9 cm. PH2015:0002:019

p. 49. View of a collage for the industrialized housing prototypes: AH-Gia Houses, 1993–1996 (AP164.S1.1993.D11). Digital print, 20 × 24.9 cm. PH2015:0002:001

p. 50. View of a print for IKEA Alcorcón, Madrid, 1992–1996. (AP164.S1.1994.D1). Digital print, 20.1 × 29.9 cm. PH2015:0002:054

November 2014

Kersten Geers and David Van Severen discuss objects they encounter during their research residency in the Ábalos&Herreros archive.

  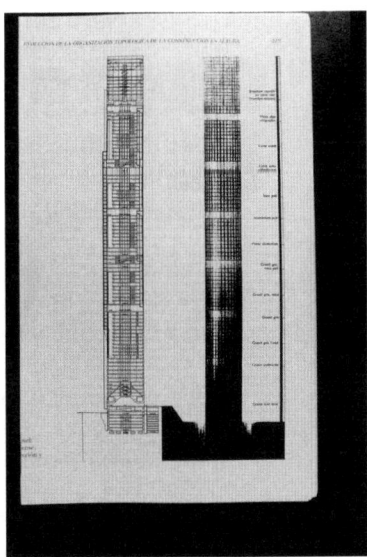 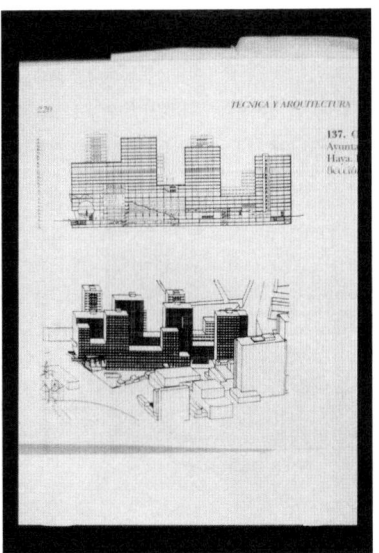

David Van Severen: We are investigating the fascination of Ábalos&Herreros with an industrial approach to architecture. Kersten studied with them in Madrid in 1997 and 1998, and I was there in 2000, which was the time at which their interests resulted in Usera library and in other projects such as the gymnastics pavilion in Retiro Park.

In the archive, we found some of the teaching material that we encountered during our studies with Ábalos&Herreros. A set of teaching slides shows projects that were references for them and that illustrate their fascination with American towers and typical plans, as well as with contemporary architecture.

The set of slides includes images of Jean Nouvel's Tour sans fins, the John Hancock Center by SOM, Dominique Perrault's Hôtel industriel and projects by Rem Koolhaas, among others. Ábalos&Herreros had this almost technocratic interest in architecture, and in the way it can consist of a composition of different found elements.

Above, from left to right:
Dominqiue Perrault.
Hôtel industriel, Paris, 1986–1990.
Black-and-white slide, 5 × 5 cm.
AP164.S2.SS3.D1.ARCH270795

Bruce Graham and Fazlur Khan (SOM). John Hancock Center, Chicago, 1965–1969.
Black-and-white slide, 5 × 5 cm.
AP164.S2.SS3.D1.ARCH270842

Jean Nouvel. Tour sans fins, Paris, 1988. Colour slide, 5 × 5 cm.
AP164.S2.SS3.D1.ARCH270796

OMA. City Hall, The Hague, 1987.
Colour slide, 5 × 5 cm.
AP164.S2.SS3.D1.ARCH270797

DVS: We were not aware that Ábalos&Herreros made models, so finding a model of Usera library in the archive was a surprise. The model shows that the production of Ábalos&Herreros essentially consisted of boxes, but beautiful boxes.

Kersten Geers: We are looking at different boxes during our research here, and Usera is probably the most sublime, the most precise and the best designed of these projects. But the material we found in the archive is quite uneven. We spent a great deal of time with the digital material because there are many CAD drawings, which were fundamental to the way Ábalos&Herreros approached architecture.

It is therefore fascinating to find a building represented in such a precise model. It is probably a presentation model, perhaps done for a competition. The model shows the building itself as well as the landscaping, which is extremely simple and pragmatic. Some of the panels have fallen off. They are fixed panels meant for sun protection and they seem to be able to be opened and closed. They suggest movability, but actually they are not movable: there is a certain promise of a building in the model.

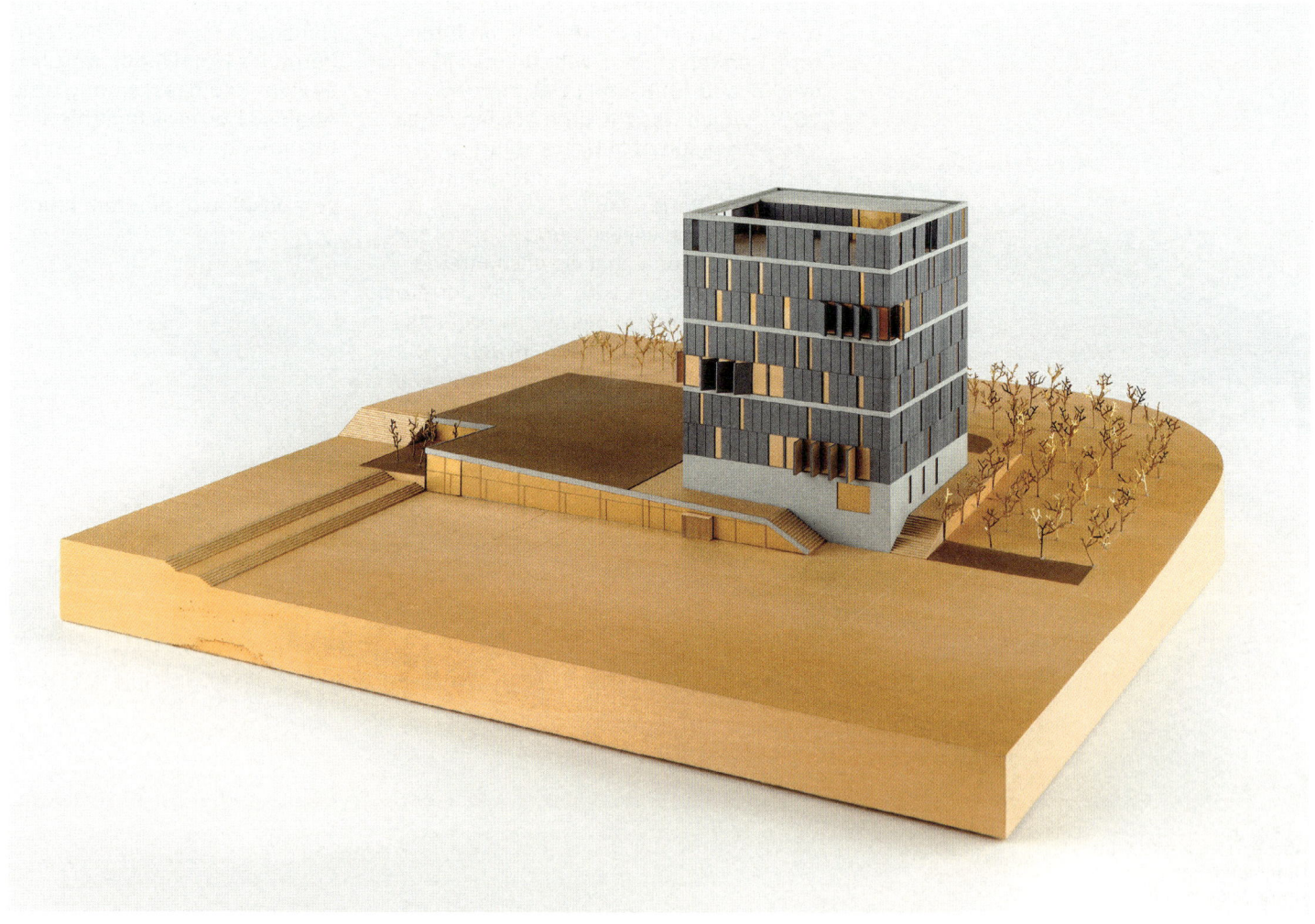

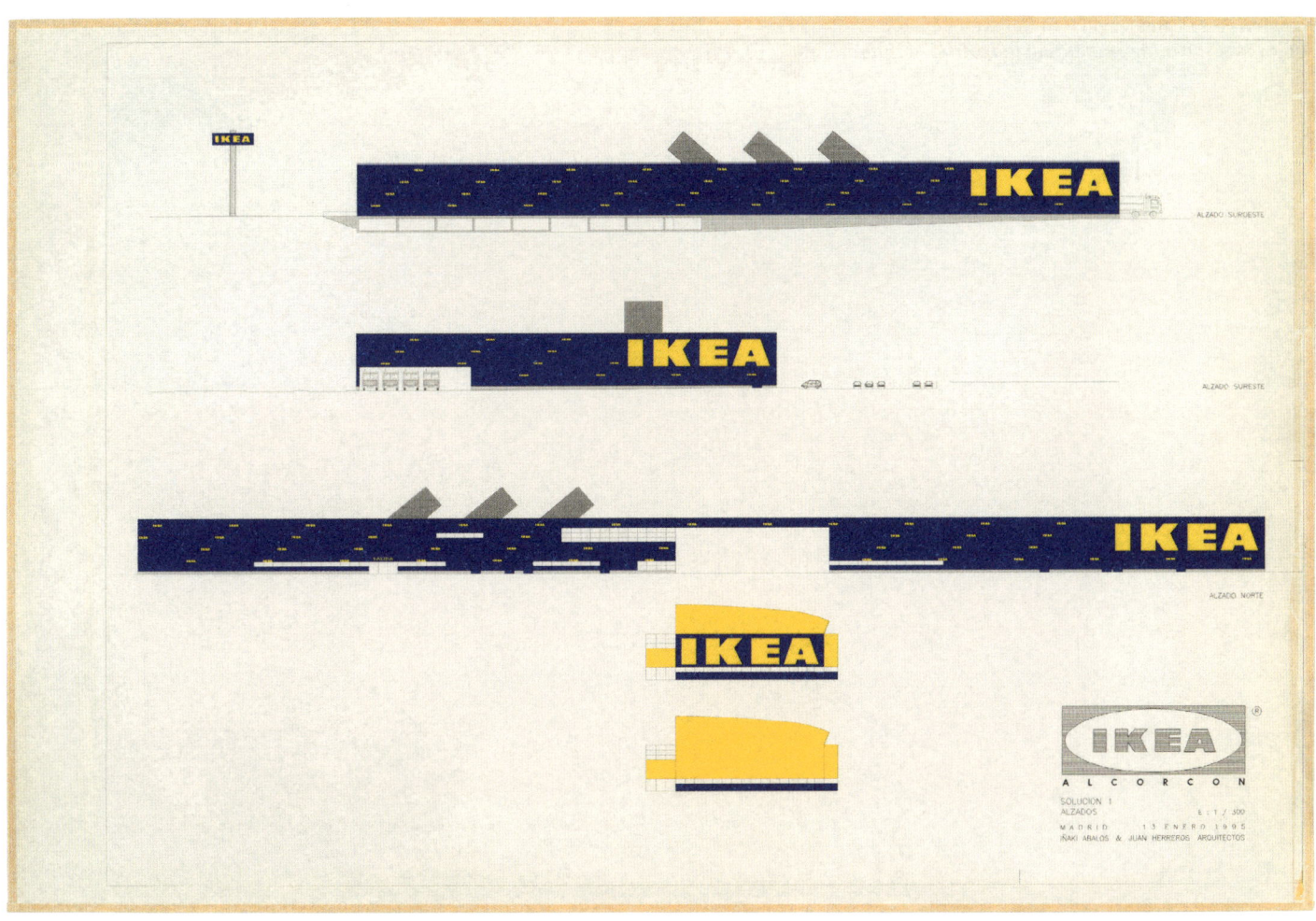

KG: On the other end of the spectrum there is a set of prints of an IKEA industrial box. The prints present an interesting negotiation between elements that make an IKEA—such as the colour scheme and the big letters—as well as a rethinking of the simple box. The set includes a series of studies of the roof line and the objects on the roof, as well as a version with the word *IKEA* printed in small type in a repeating pattern.

DVS: At first we thought these documents were collages, but in fact they are prints that have a 1990s ink-jet quality. They are therefore versions of something that Ábalos&Herreros made on the computer.

KG: The prints are quite different from what we knew of the work of Ábalos& Herreros. Both David and I studied with Iñaki and Juan at around the time that Usera library was designed, so we know that project very well. It became emblematic of their work, whereas this IKEA box, developed at roughly the same time, shows how Ábalos&Herreros entered the most banal of building programs, which was historically not the subject of focused architectural production. Seen somewhat romantically, their technique has something in common with an Ed Ruscha perspective, in which the front facade becomes the representation of the building. From all the banality of word, volume and colour, it may be possible to make something special.

Opposite: Model of Usera library, 1997. Wood, plastic, paper, metal and cardboard, 30.8 × 71.5 × 64 cm.
AP164.S1.1995.D1.ARCH269169

Above: Print for IKEA Alcorcón, 1995. Colour ink-jet print, 63.1 × 91.9 cm.
AP164.S1.1994.D1.ARCH267558

**Kersten Geers and David Van Severen develop
their research in the exhibition** *Industrial Architecture*.

Ábalos&Herreros
selected by

Kersten Geers and
David Van Severen

12 March – 17 May
2015

Industrial Architecture

Industrial Architecture
Material included in the exhibition

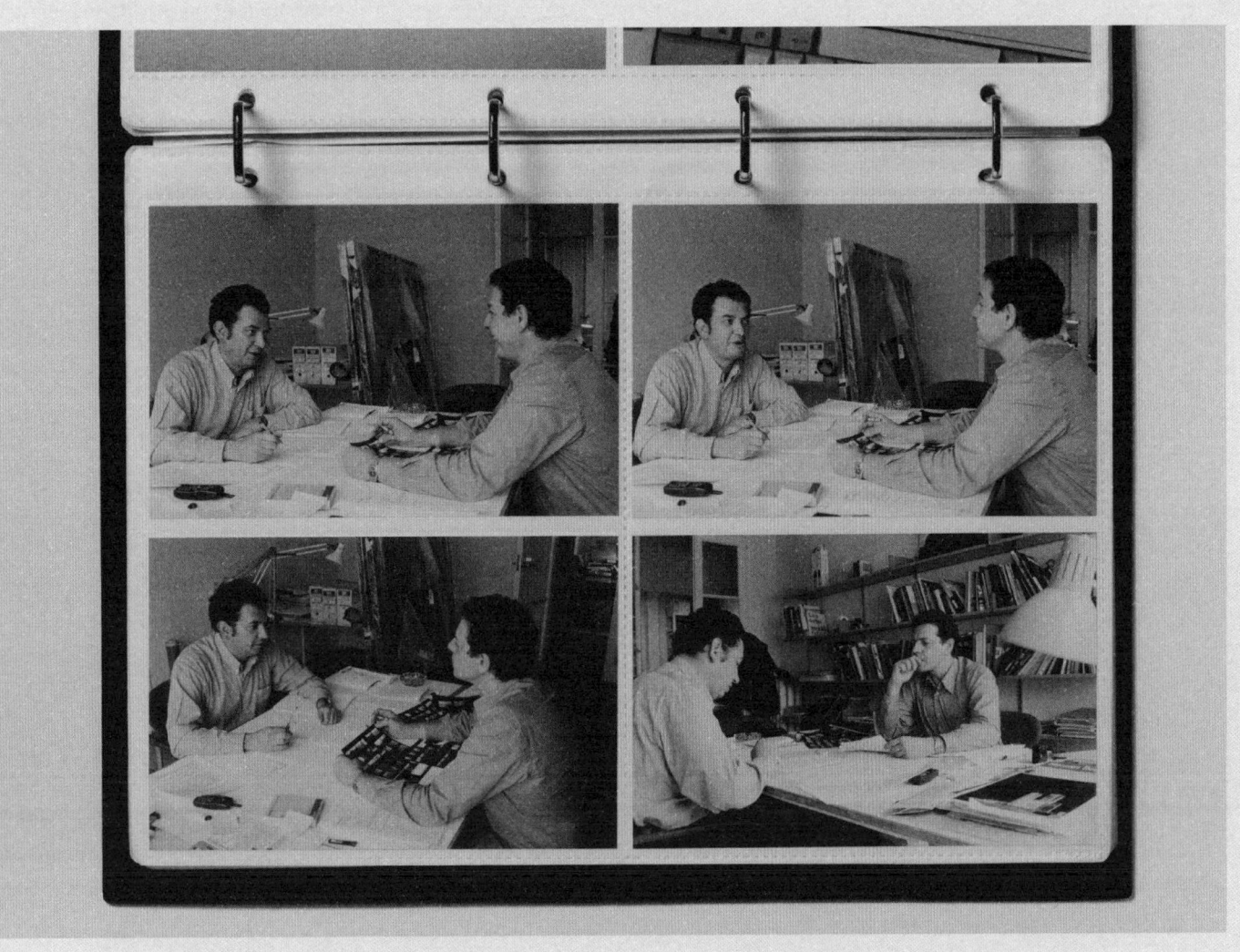

Iñaki Ábalos and Juan Herreros
in their office, Madrid, 1999
AP164.S3.D2.ARCH270451

Lewis Baltz
From the series *The New Industrial Parks Near Irvine, California*

Three gelatin silver prints
1974

*East wall, Western Carpet Mills,
1231 Warner, Tustin, California*
PH2001:0155

*South wall, unoccupied industrial structure,
16812 Milliken, Irvine, California*
PH2001:0157

*West wall, unoccupied industrial structure,
20 Airway Drive, Costa Mesa, California*
PH2001:0183

*East wall, Western Carpet Mills,
1231 Warner, Tustin, California*
PH2001:0155

Stefano Graziani
From the series *Proofs of Relevance*

Twenty-seven views of selected objects from the Ábalos&Herreros archive
Digital prints
2014
PH2015:2001:001-056

Commissioned by the Canadian Centre for Architecture, Montréal
Gift of the artist

View of a photomontage for the environmental education centre and offices, Arico, Tenerife, 1998–2001 (AP164.S1.1998.D1)
PH2015:0002:046

CAD drawings
Selected projects

Head office for the Savings Bank of Granada, 1992
AP164.S1.1992.D4

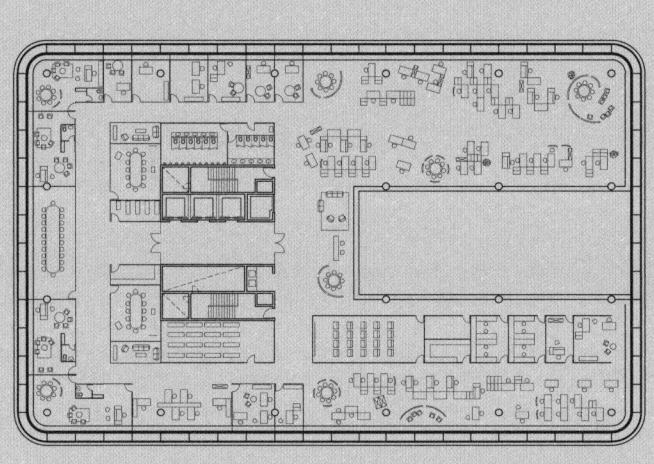

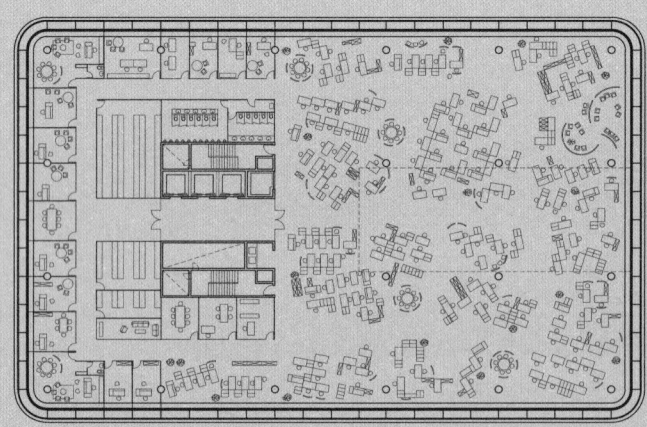

078   1:500

CAD drawings
Selected projects

#042 *Ordenación de la Plaza de Castilla*
     Planning proposal for Plaza de Castilla, Madrid, 1986
     Facsimile
     AP164.S1.1986.D6

#056 *Centro de cálculo para Telefónica*
     Data centre for Telefónica, Madrid, 1989
     Facsimile
     AP164.S1.1989.D1

#058 *Edificio de oficinas de RENFE*
     RENFE office building, Madrid, 1989–1991
     AP164.S1.1989.D3

#059 *Vivienda y ciudad, avenida Diagonal*
     Housing and the City competition, Avinguda Diagonal,
     Barcelona, 1989
     Facsimile
     AP164.S1.1989.D4

#063 *Polideportivo Parquesol*
     Parquesol sports hall, Valladolid, 1990
     Facsimile
     AP164.S1.1990.D2

#064 *Edificio administrativo para el Ministerio del interior*
     Administrative building for the Ministry of the Interior,
     Madrid, 1990–1992
     AP164.S1.1990.D3

#067 *Polideportivo Madrigral de las Altas Torres*
     Sports hall, Madrigal de las Altas Torres, Ávila, 1990
     AP164.S1.1990.D6

#078 *Caja de Ahorros de Granada*
     Head office for the Savings Bank of Granada, 1992
     AP164.S1.1992.D4

#083 *Ordenación del área de Abandoibarra*
     Planning proposal for the Abandoibarra area, Bilbao, 1993
     AP164.S1.1993.D5

#085 *Unidad residencial de Barajas*
     Housing block, Barajas, Madrid, 1993
     AP164.S1.1993.D7

#089 *Prototipos de vivienda industrializada: Casas AH-Gia*
     Industrialized housing prototypes: AH-Gia Houses,
     1993–1996
     AP164.S1.1993.D11

#090 *IKEA Alcorcón*
     IKEA Alcorcón, Madrid, 1992–1996
     AP164.S1.1994.D1

#094 *Biblioteca de Usera*
     Usera library, Madrid, 1995–2003
     AP164.S1.1995.D1

#098 *Facultad de filosofía y ciencias de la educación, Cáceres*
     Faculty of Philosophy and Education Science, Cáceres, 1996
     AP164.S1.1996.D3

#099 *Planta de reciclaje de residuos urbanos de Valdemingómez*
     Recycling plant for urban waste, Valdemingómez, Madrid,
     1996–1999
     AP164.S1.1996.D4

#111 *Centro de control y aula medioambiental de Arico*
     Environmental education centre and offices, Arico, Tenerife,
     1998–2001
     AP164.S1.1998.D1

#117 *Edificio de servicios para la Universidad de Extremadura*
     University of Extremadura service building, Mérida, 1999–2001
     AP164.S1.1999.D4

#123 *El Mirador: torre mixta en la Bahía de Algeciras*
     El Mirador: mixed-used tower on the Bay of Gibraltar,
     Algeciras, 1999
     AP164.S1.1999.D10

#125 *Instituto en Almería*
     Secondary school, Almería, 2000
     AP164.S1.2000.D1

#127 *Pabellón de gimnasia en el parque del Retiro*
     Gymnastics pavilion in Retiro Park, Madrid, c. 2000–2003
     AP164.S1.2000.D3

#130 *Planta de biometanización y compostaje de residuos urbanos*
     Biomethanation and composting plant, Pinto, 2000–2003
     AP164.S1.2000.D6

#131 *Einsteinet, edificio de oficinas y show-room*
     Einsteinet, office building and showroom, Hamburg, 2000
     AP164.S1.2000.D7

#132 *Centro de enseñanza secundaria obligatoria de Fuente
     de Cantos*
     Secondary school, Fuente de Cantos, Badajoz, 2000
     AP164.S1.2000.D8.SD4

#142 *Plaza y torre Woermann*
     Woermann Plaza and Tower, Las Palmas de Gran Canaria,
     2001–2005
     AP164.S1.2001.D7

#144 *Centro de enseñanza secundaria*
     Secondary school, Tiétar, Cáceres, 1999–2001
     AP164.S1.2001.D9

#146 *Torres mixtas bioclimáticas en el Humedal de Salburua*
     Environmental mixed-use towers in the Salburua wetlands,
     Vitoria-Gasteiz, 2002–2006
     AP164.S1.2002.D2

#149 *Centro de reciclaje y revaloración*
     Recycling centre, Logroño, 2002
     AP164.S1.2002.D5

#150 *Recualificación de la planta de compostaje La Paloma*
     Renovation of La Paloma Composting Plant, Valdemingómez,
     Madrid, 2002
     AP164.S1.2002.D6

#152 *Viviendas para jóvenes en Sant Andreu*
     Youth housing in Sant Andreu, Barcelona, 2002
     AP164.S1.2002.D8

#158 *Centro de Cirugía de Mínima Invasión*
     Minimally Invasive Surgery Centre, Cáceres, 2002
     AP164.S1.2002.D13

#161 *New Museum de Arte Contemporáneo*
     New Museum of Contemporary Art, New York, 2003
     AP164.S1.2003.D1

#176 *Laboratorios de ciencias moleculares para la Universidad
     de Puerto Rico*
     Molecular sciences laboratories for the University of
     Puerto Rico, San Juan, 2003–2004
     AP164.S1.2003.D13

#182 *Polideportivo*
     Sports hall, Molina de Segura, Murcia, 2004
     AP164.S1.2004.D4

#187 *EPFL learning centre*
     EPFL learning centre, Lausanne, 2004
     AP164.S1.2004.D9

Teaching material and illustrations used by Iñaki Ábalos and Juan Herreros
Selection of photographic slides

Viewing device designed by Ábalos&Herreros for the
Third Biennial of Spanish Architecture and Urbanism,
Comillas and Madrid, 1996–1997

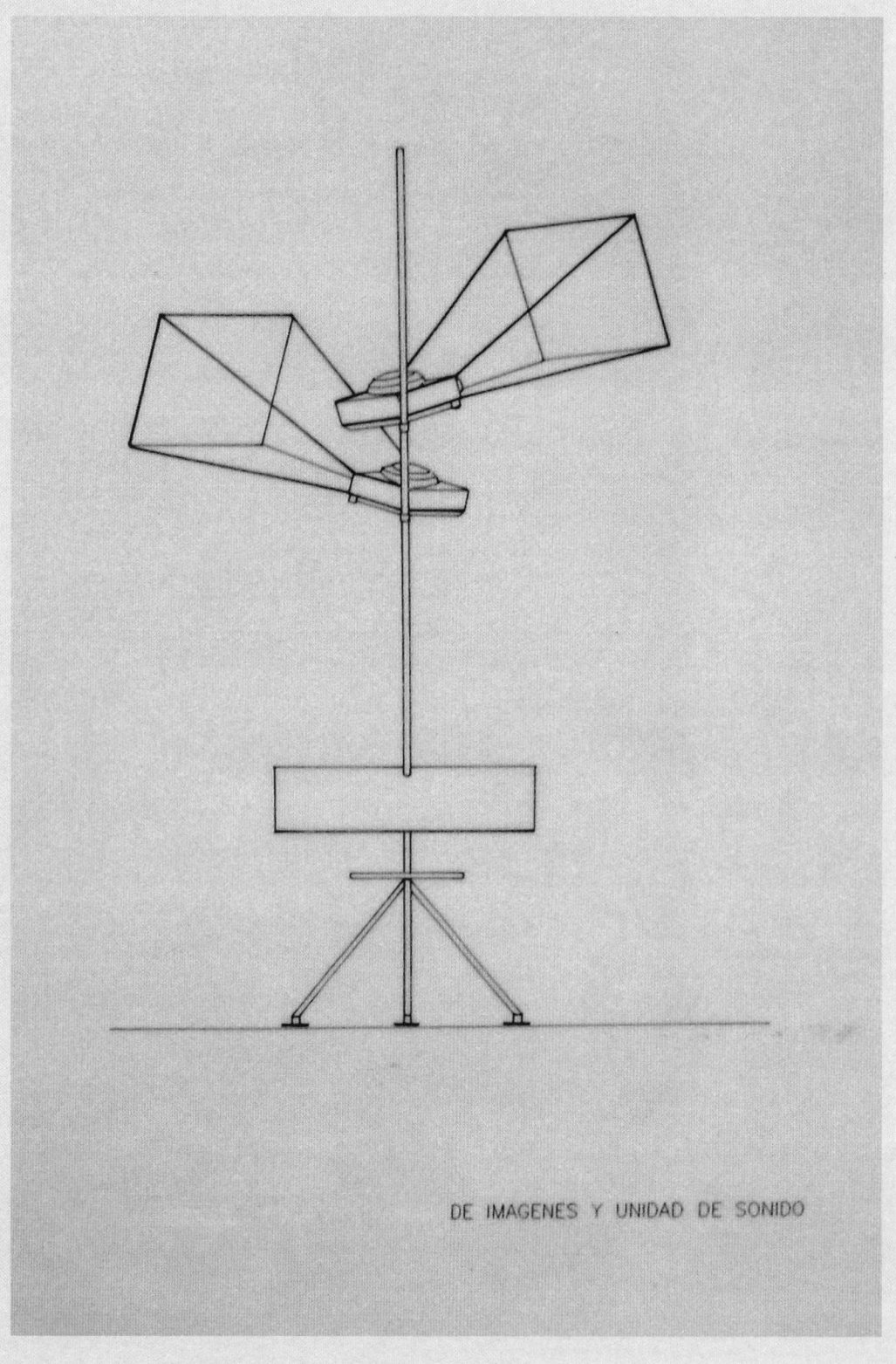

Teaching material and illustrations used by Iñaki Ábalos and Juan Herreros
Selection of photographic slides

European and American shopping centres

Erich Mendelsohn
Rudolf Petersdorff department store, Wrocław, 1927–1929
AP164.S3.D2.ARCH270818

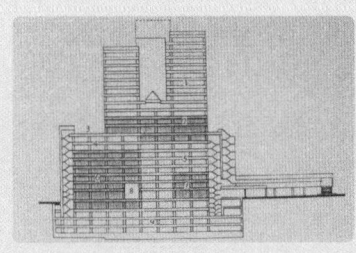

Unidentified project
AP164.S3.D2.ARCH270829

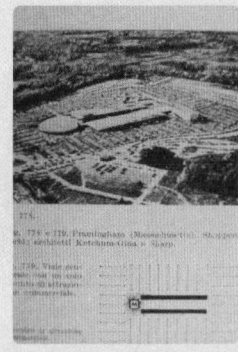

Ketchum, Gina & Sharp
Shoppers' World, Framingham, Massachusetts, 1949–1951
AP164.S3.D2.ARCH270839

Marcel Breuer
De Bijenkorf department store, Rotterdam, 1955–1957
AP164.S3.D2.ARCH270816

Franco Albini and Franca Helg
La Rinascente department store, Rome, 1957–1961
AP164.S3.D2.ARCH270817

John Graham Jr.
Yorkdale Shopping Centre, Toronto, 1964
AP164.S3.D2.ARCH270855

César Pelli
Pacific Design Center, Los Angeles, 1975
AP164.S3.D2.ARCH270854

Frank Gehry
Santa Monica Place, 1979–1981
AP164.S3.D2.ARCH270853

James Wines / Sculpture in the Environment (SITE)
BEST Products Word Project, 1974
AP164.S3.D2.ARCH270851

Robert Venturi, John Rauch and Denise Scott Brown
BEST Products Showroom, Langhorne, Pennsylvania, 1973–1979
AP164.S3.D2.ARCH270852

James Wines / Sculpture in the Environment (SITE)
Anti-Sign BEST Products Showroom, Ashland, Virginia, 1978–1979
AP164.S3.D2.ARCH270856

James Wines / Sculpture in the Environment (SITE)
BEST Products Tilt Showroom, Towson, Maryland, 1978
AP164.S3.D2.ARCH270837

Alejandro de la Sota
Aviaco Airlines Headquarters, Madrid, 1975
AP164.S3.D2.ARCH270826

Aldo Rossi
Centro Torri shopping centre, Parma, 1985–1988
AP164.S3.D2.ARCH270838

Teaching material and illustrations used by Iñaki Ábalos and Juan Herreros
Selection of photographic slides

Illustrations from the book *Técnica y arquitectura en la ciudad contemporánea, 1950–1990*
(Editorial Nerea, 1992), by Iñaki Ábalos and Juan Herreros

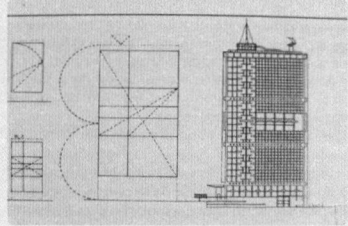

Le Corbusier
Cartesian Skyscraper, Algiers, 1929
AP164.S2.SS3.D1.ARCH270776

Louis Kahn and Anne Tyng
City Tower, Philadelphia, 1952–1957
AP164.S2.SS3.D1.ARCH270777

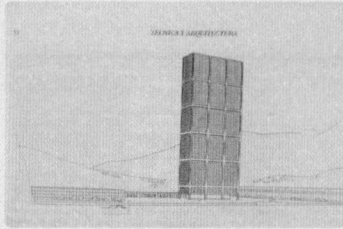

Myron Goldsmith
Concrete skyscraper from his master's thesis, 1953
AP164.S2.SS3.D1.ARCH270778

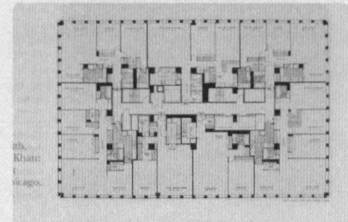

Myron Goldsmith, Bruce Graham and Fazlur Khan (SOM)
Chestnut-DeWitt apartments, Chicago, 1961–1965
AP164.S2.SS3.D1.ARCH270779

Myron Goldsmith, Bruce Graham and Fazlur Khan (SOM)
Brunswick Building, Chicago, 1962–1966
AP164.S2.SS3.D1.ARCH270780

Bruce Graham and Fazlur Khan (SOM)
John Hancock Center, Chicago, 1965–1969
AP164.S2.SS3.D1.ARCH270842

Fazlur Khan
Diagram of heights for structural systems, 1969
AP164.S2.SS3.D1.ARCH270844

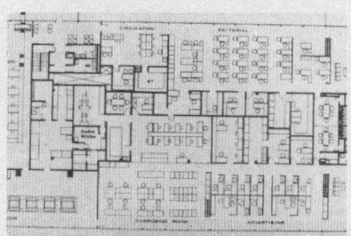

Myron Goldsmith
The Republic newspaper plant, Columbus, 1971
AP164.S2.SS3.D1.ARCH270803

Francisco Javier Sáenz de Oiza
Bank of Bilbao Tower, Madrid, 1971–1981
AP164.S2.SS3.D1.ARCH270782

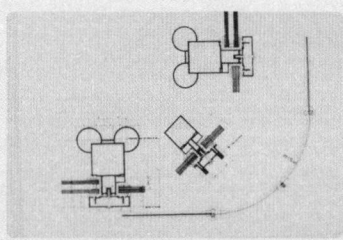

Francisco Javier Sáenz de Oiza
Bank of Bilbao Tower, Madrid, 1971–1981
AP164.S2.SS3.D1.ARCH270781

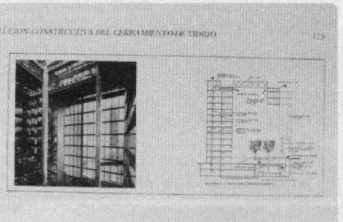

Kevin Roche and John Dinkeloo
Ford Foundation Building, New York, 1963–1968
AP164.S2.SS3.D1.ARCH270783

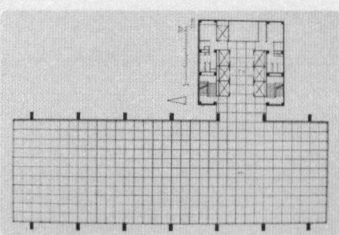

Bruce Graham, Walter Netsch and Fazlur Khan (SOM)
Inland Steel Building, Chicago, 1954–1957
AP164.S2.SS3.D1.ARCH270843

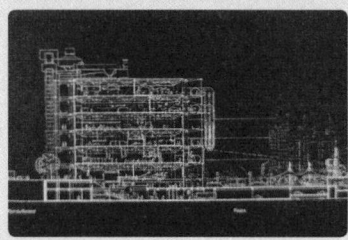

Renzo Piano and Richard Rogers
Centre Georges Pompidou, Paris, 1971–1977
AP164.S2.SS3.D1.ARCH270784

Frank Lloyd Wright
Larkin Building, Buffalo, 1904–1906
AP164.S2.SS3.D1.ARCH270785

Raymond Hood
Rockefeller Center, New York, 1931–1932
AP164.S2.SS3.D1.ARCH270786

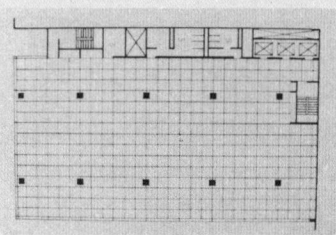

Skidmore, Owings & Merrill
Pepsi-Cola Corporation World Headquarters, New York
AP164.S2.SS3.D1.ARCH270787

Teaching material and illustrations used by Iñaki Ábalos and Juan Herreros
Selection of photographic slides

Illustrations from the book *Técnica y arquitectura en la ciudad contemporánea, 1950–1990*
(Editorial Nerea, 1992), by Iñaki Ábalos and Juan Herreros

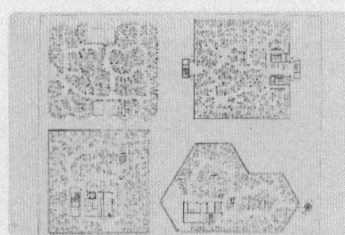

Quickborner Team
Typical plans of offices,
n.d.
AP164.S2.SS3.D1.ARCH270789

Tiffany Industries
Grouping of individual workstations,
n.d.
AP164.S2.SS3.D1.ARCH270790

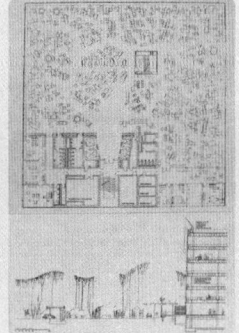

Walter Henn
Osram GmbH Administration Building,
Munich, 1962–1965
AP164.S2.SS3.D1.ARCH270791

Starrett & Van Vleck
Downtown Athletic Club, New York,
1931
AP164.S2.SS3.D1.ARCH270792

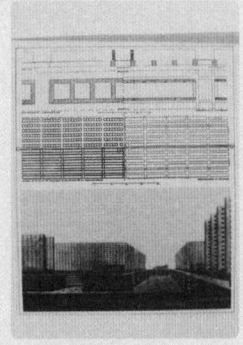

Ludwig Hilberseimer
Vertical City, 1924
AP164.S2.SS3.D1.ARCH270793

Herzog & de Meuron
Berlin Zentrum, 1990
AP164.S2.SS3.D1.ARCH270794

Dominqiue Perrault
Hôtel industriel, Paris, 1986–1990
AP164.S2.SS3.D1.ARCH270795

Jean Nouvel
Tour sans fins, Paris, 1988
AP164.S2.SS3.D1.ARCH270796

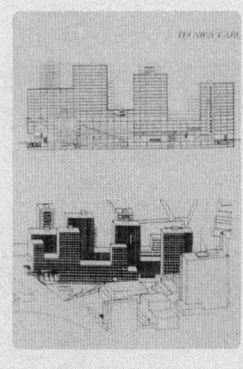

OMA
City Hall, The Hague, 1987
AP164.S2.SS3.D1.ARCH270797

Teaching material and illustrations used by Iñaki Ábalos and Juan Herreros
Selection of photographic slides

A survey of modern architectural projects (1922–1991)

Mies van der Rohe
Glass Skyscraper, Berlin, 1922
AP164.S3.D2.ARCH270810

Mies van der Rohe
Concrete Office Building, Berlin, 1923
AP164.S3.D2.ARCH270812

Le Corbusier
Cité d'affaires, Algiers, 1938–1942
AP164.S3.D2.ARCH270831

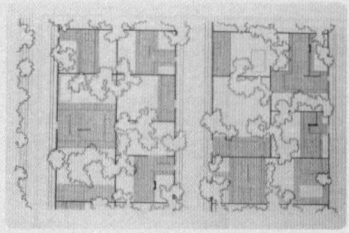

Mies van der Rohe
Courtyard housing study, 1931
AP164.S3.D2.ARCH270813

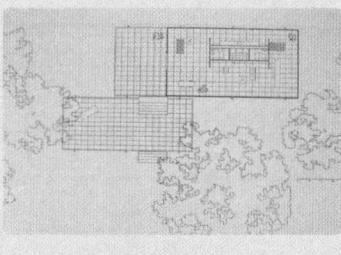

Mies van der Rohe
Farnsworth House, Plano, Illinois, 1945–1951
AP164.S3.D2.ARCH270801

Mies van der Rohe
Lake Shore Drive Apartments, Chicago, 1948–1951
AP164.S3.D2.ARCH270799

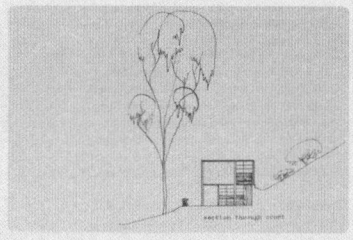

Charles and Ray Eames
Case Study House no. 8, Pacific Palisades, California, 1945–1949
AP164.S3.D2.ARCH270824

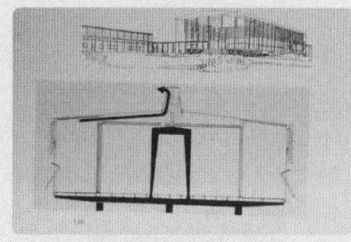

Jean Prouvé
Maison tropicale, 1948–1949
AP164.S3.D2.ARCH270807

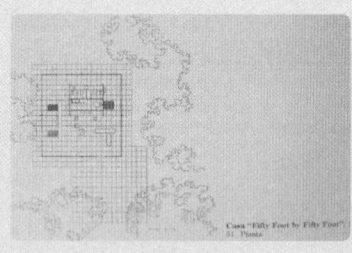

Mies van der Rohe
50 × 50 House, 1950–1952
AP164.S3.D2.ARCH270815

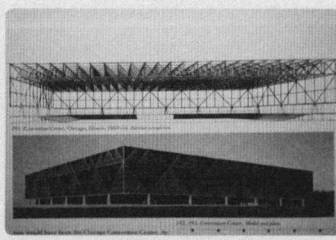

Mies van der Rohe
Chicago Convention Center, 1953–1954
AP164.S3.D2.ARCH273086

Myron Goldsmith (SOM)
United Airlines Hangar, San Francisco, 1956–1958
AP164.S3.D2.ARCH270800

R. Buckminster Fuller
Cornell Pinecone Plydome, Ithaca, New York, 1957
AP164.S3.D2.ARCH270850

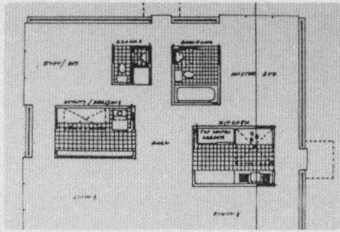

Alison and Peter Smithson
Retirement house, Kent, 1959
AP164.S3.D2.ARCH270848

Alison and Peter Smithson
Upper Lawn Pavilion, Wiltshire, 1959–1962
AP164.S3.D2.ARCH270845

Unidentified project
AP164.S3.D2.ARCH270806

Unidentified project
AP164.S3.D2.ARCH270805

Teaching material and illustrations used by Iñaki Ábalos and Juan Herreros
Selection of photographic slides

A survey of modern architectural projects (1922–1991)

Alejandro de la Sota
Maravillas Gymnasium, Madrid,
1960–1962
AP164.S3.D2.ARCH270823

Alejandro de la Sota
Maravillas Gymnasium, Madrid,
1960–1962
AP164.S3.D2.ARCH270822

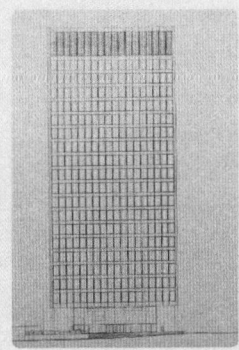

Mies van der Rohe
Mansion House Square, London,
1962–1985
AP164.S3.D2.ARCH270814

Kevin Roche and John Dinkeloo
Ford Foundation Building, New York,
1963–1968
AP164.S3.D2.ARCH270857

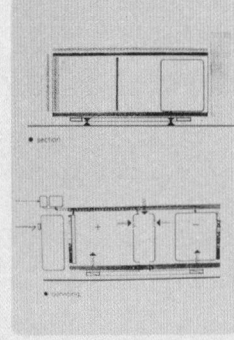

Alison and Peter Smithson
Steel Housing Competition, 1966
AP164.S3.D2.ARCH270849

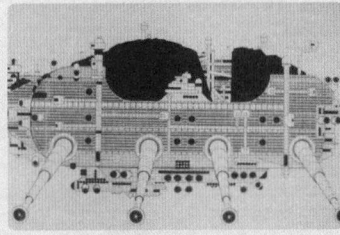

Ron Herron / Archigram
Walking City, 1964
AP164.S3.D2.ARCH270841

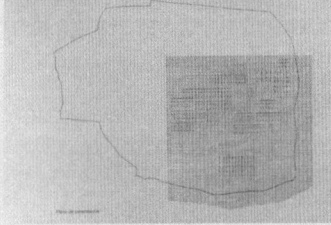

Alejandro de la Sota
Residential College for the Provincial
Savings Bank, Orense, Spain, 1966–1967
AP164.S3.D2.ARCH270859

Kevin Roche and John Dinkeloo
College Life Insurance Building,
Indianapolis, 1967–1971
AP164.S3.D2.ARCH270858

Frank Gehry
Davis Studio and Residence, Malibu,
1968–1972
AP164.S3.D2.ARCH270825

Ron Herron / Archigram
Instant City, 1970
AP164.S3.D2.ARCH270847

Renzo Piano and Richard Rogers
Centre Georges Pompidou, Paris,
1971–1977
AP164.S3.D2.ARCH270846

Norman Foster
Sainsbury Centre for Visual Arts,
Norwich, 1974–1978
AP164.S3.D2.ARCH270834

Norman Foster
Sainsbury Centre for Visual Arts,
Norwich, 1974–1978
AP164.S3.D2.ARCH270836

Robert Venturi, Denise Scott Brown
and Steven Izenour
"Recommendation for a Monument"
from *Learning From Las Vegas,* 1977
AP164.S3.D2.ARCH270827

Teaching material and illustrations used by Iñaki Ábalos and Juan Herreros
Selection of photographic slides

A survey of modern architectural projects (1922–1991)

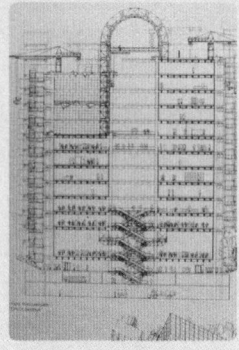

Richard Rogers
Lloyd's of London, London, 1978–1986
AP164.S3.D2.ARCH270809

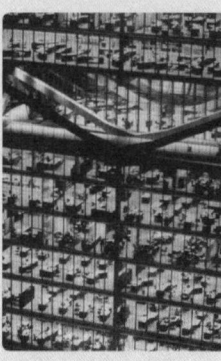

Norman Foster
Hongkong and Shanghai Bank
Headquarters, Hong Kong, 1979–1986
AP164.S3.D2.ARCH270835

John Hejduk
Berlin Masque, Berlin, 1982
AP164.S3.D2.ARCH270840

Alejandro de la Sota
Housing development, Alcúdia,
Mallorca, 1983–1984
AP164.S3.D2.ARCH270821

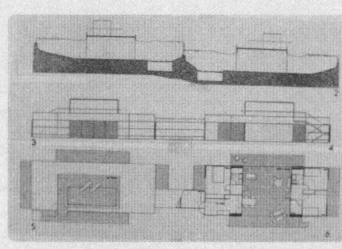

Alejandro de la Sota
Housing development, Alcúdia,
Mallorca, 1983–1984
AP164.S3.D2.ARCH270819

Jean Nouvel
Nemausus I, Nîmes, 1985–1987
AP164.S3.D2.ARCH270830

Philippe Starck
Asahi Superdry Hall, Tokyo, 1989
AP164.S3.D2.ARCH270828

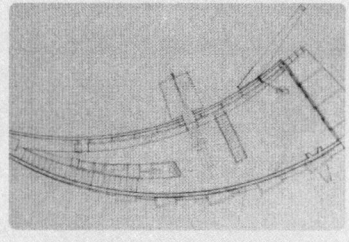

Diller + Scofidio
Slow House, Long Island, 1991
AP164.S3.D2.ARCH270833

Industrial Architecture
Kersten Geers and David Van Severen

The work of Ábalos & Herreros is a conscious mirror of architecture and time. Though their practice started in the mid-1980s, it was ultimately the 1990s that gave the work its shape and its *raison d'être*. More than any other firm, Ábalos & Herreros excelled in pragmatic reproduction. With the conviction that architecture as a cultural practice is successful only when it reflects the world it inhabits, they became masters of emulation. Their practice tackled the problems of production (of culture) through reproduction (of the world).

    Their work has to be understood as an exaggeration of architecture as industry, an understanding of the fragile balance at the outer edge of worn-out modernism. Their modernism is reduced to a set of signifiers rescued from the debris of metropolitanism and post-formal architecture of the 1990s: fucked-up pragmatism, a full economy of means. This careful architecture of economy consciously avoids being architecture altogether. As an advanced form of white noise, it is everything: it is the world.

    The projects act as the negative of their surroundings. In the world out there, their projects are a photographic print plate. In the tradition of what came to be known as the New Topographics, the work succeeds the more it disappears. For that reason *Industrial Architecture* has to be understood as an oxymoron of sorts. It is the incarnation of architecture as a technical DNA directly transmitted from the CAD file, an exemplary means of production of that era. References, prints, renderings and sporadic models are treated with equal weight, giving sense and direction to the work developed. The insights are fragmentary, since only in fragmented fashion does the work emerge as some kind of silent catalyst. As Lewis Baltz's *The New Industrial Parks Near Irvine, California*—which manages to document the formulaic modernism of standardized building practices, attempting to find the inherent beauty in this strange correlation between relentless industry and landscape—the work of Ábalos & Herreros seeks redemption in the unbiased embrace of technology that both constructs and negotiates our environment. They did this without compromise, only to disappear the moment somebody noticed.

Kersten Geers and David Van Severen

Opposite: Lewis Baltz. *East wall, Western Carpet Mills, 1231 Warner, Tustin, California*. From the series *The New Industrial Parks Near Irvine, California*. Gelatin silver print, 15.2 × 22.8 cm. PH2001:0155

Above: Lewis Baltz. *South wall, unoccupied industrial structure, 16812 Milliken, Irvine, California*. From the series *The New Industrial Parks Near Irvine, California*. Gelatin silver print, 15.2 × 22.8 cm. PH2001:0157

Lewis Baltz. *West wall, unoccupied industrial structure, 20 Airway Drive, Costa Mesa, California.*
From the series *The New Industrial Parks Near Irvine, California*.
Gelatin silver print, 15.2 × 22.8 cm.
PH2001:0183

Kersten Geers and David Van Severen printed AutoCAD drawings for
Ábalos&Herreros projects to display in the exhibition. Drawings are
presented here in chronological order.

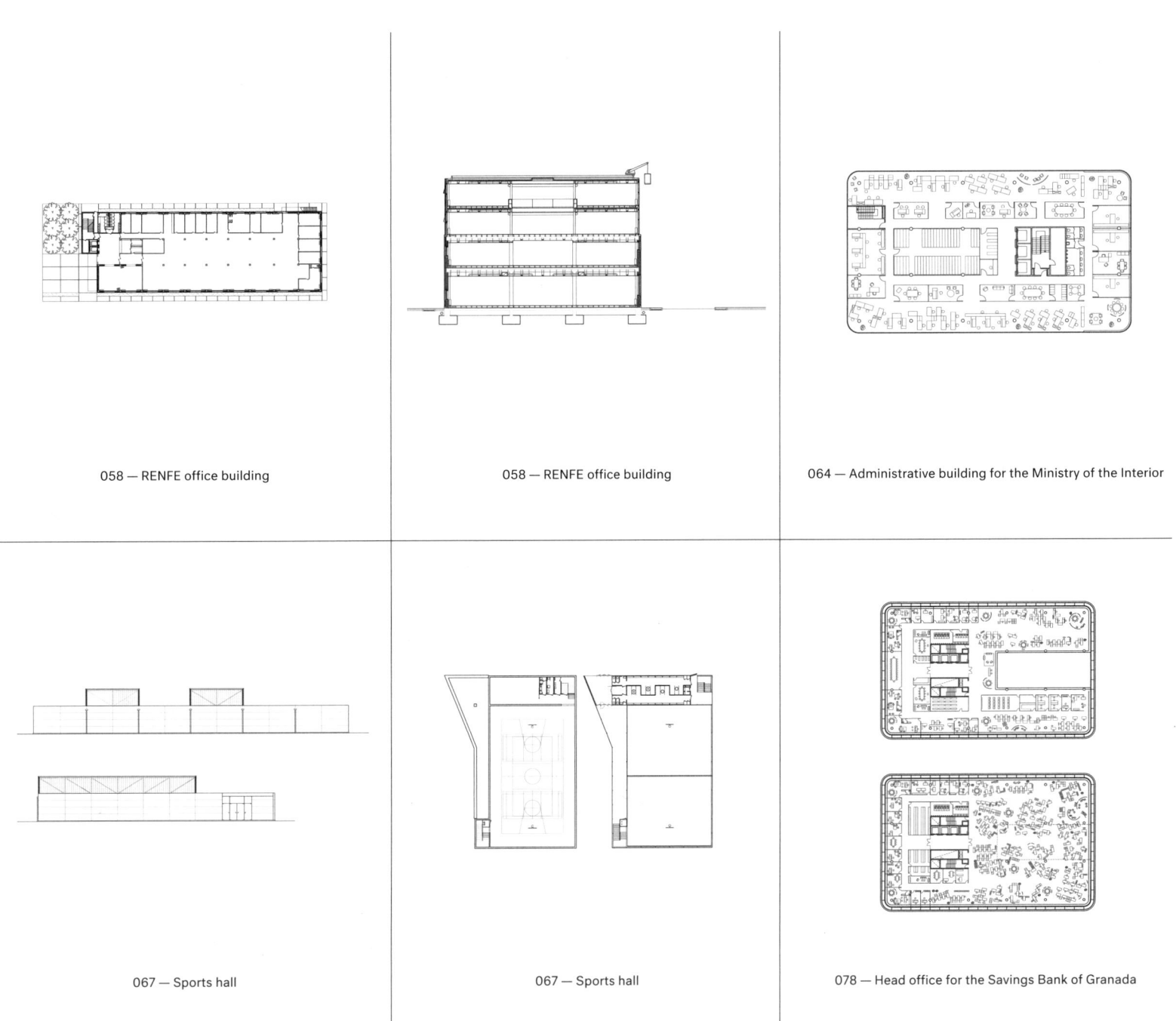

058 — RENFE office building

058 — RENFE office building

064 — Administrative building for the Ministry of the Interior

067 — Sports hall

067 — Sports hall

078 — Head office for the Savings Bank of Granada

Kersten Geers and David Van Severen

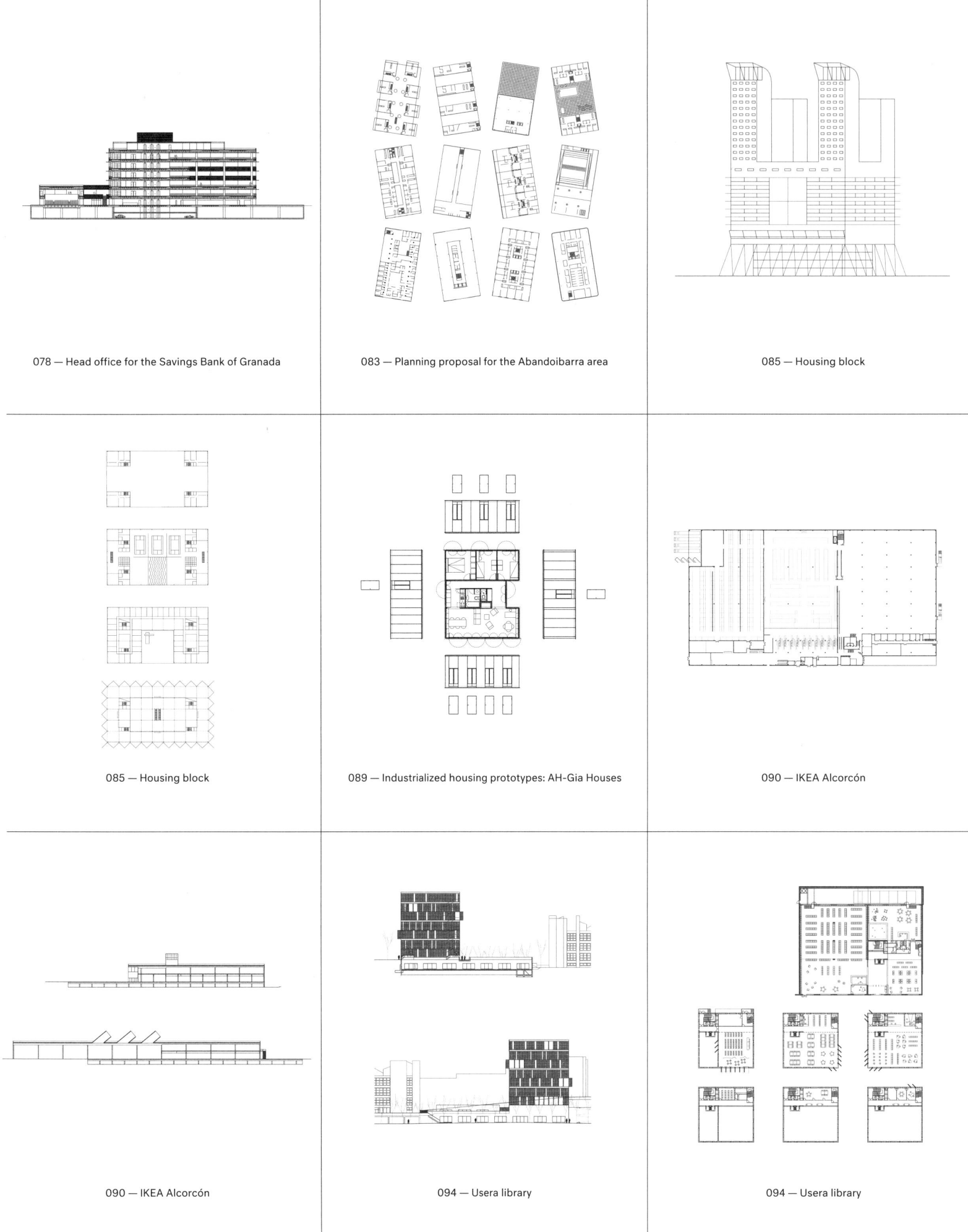

078 — Head office for the Savings Bank of Granada

083 — Planning proposal for the Abandoibarra area

085 — Housing block

085 — Housing block

089 — Industrialized housing prototypes: AH-Gia Houses

090 — IKEA Alcorcón

090 — IKEA Alcorcón

094 — Usera library

094 — Usera library

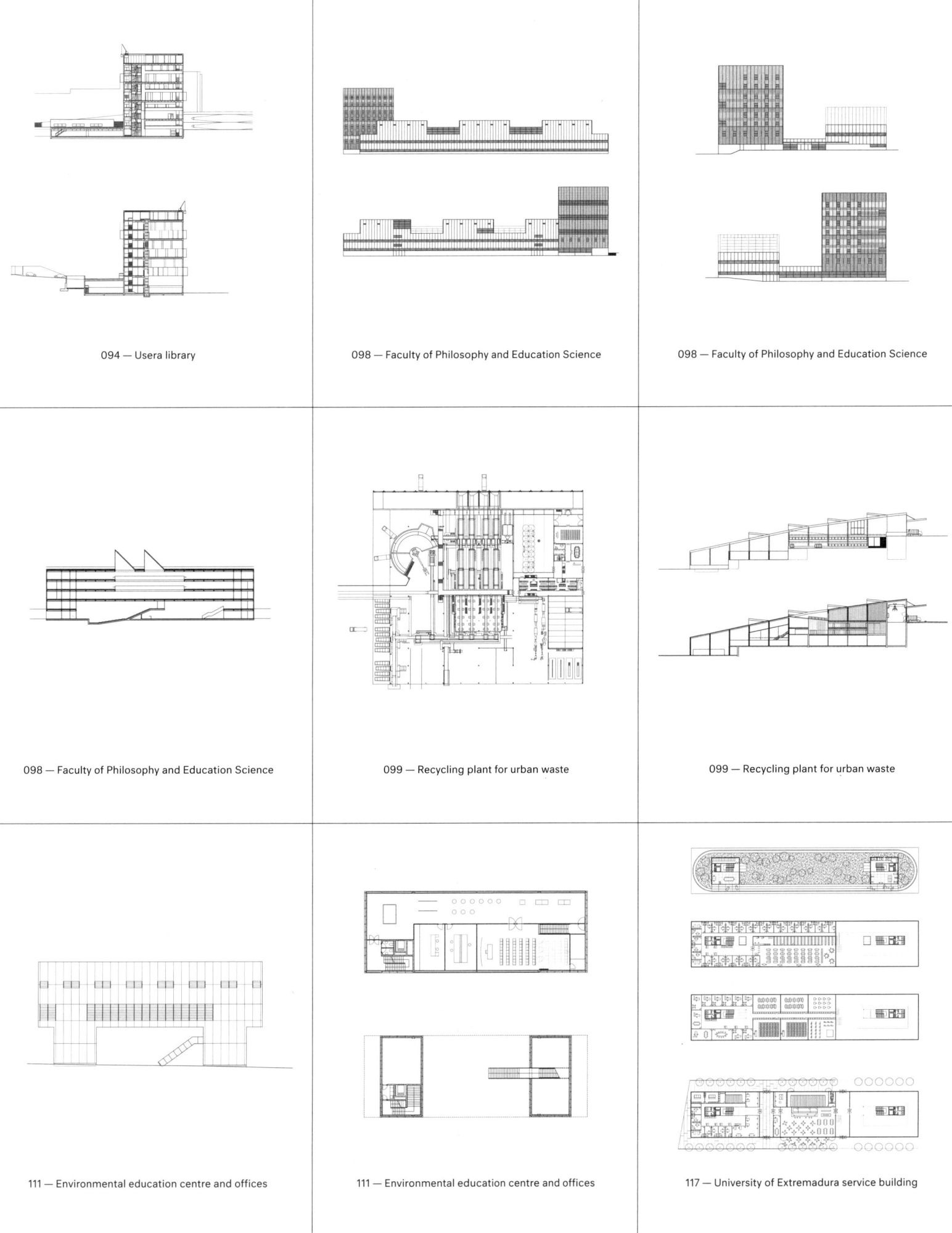

Kersten Geers and David Van Severen

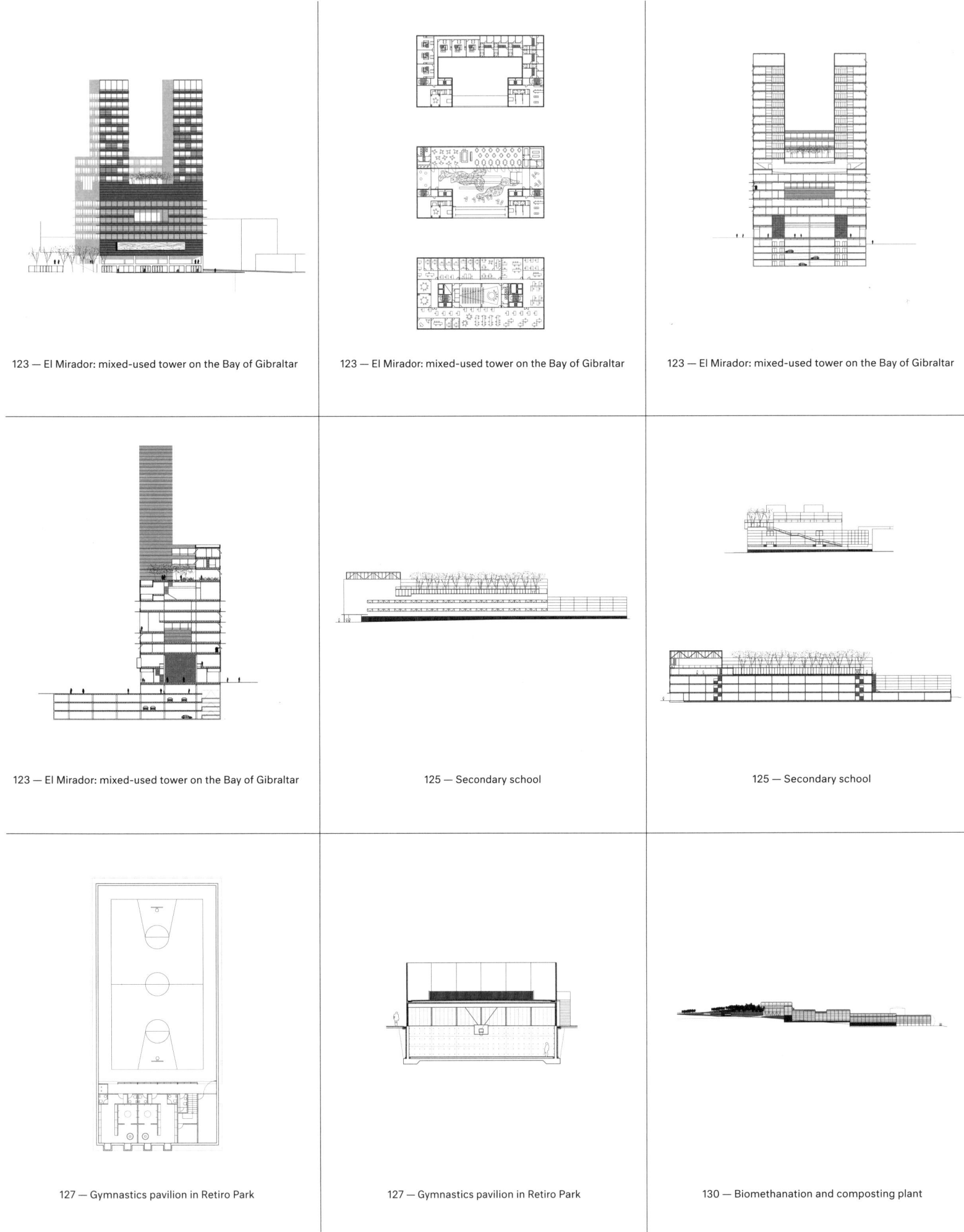

123 — El Mirador: mixed-used tower on the Bay of Gibraltar

123 — El Mirador: mixed-used tower on the Bay of Gibraltar

123 — El Mirador: mixed-used tower on the Bay of Gibraltar

123 — El Mirador: mixed-used tower on the Bay of Gibraltar

125 — Secondary school

125 — Secondary school

127 — Gymnastics pavilion in Retiro Park

127 — Gymnastics pavilion in Retiro Park

130 — Biomethanation and composting plant

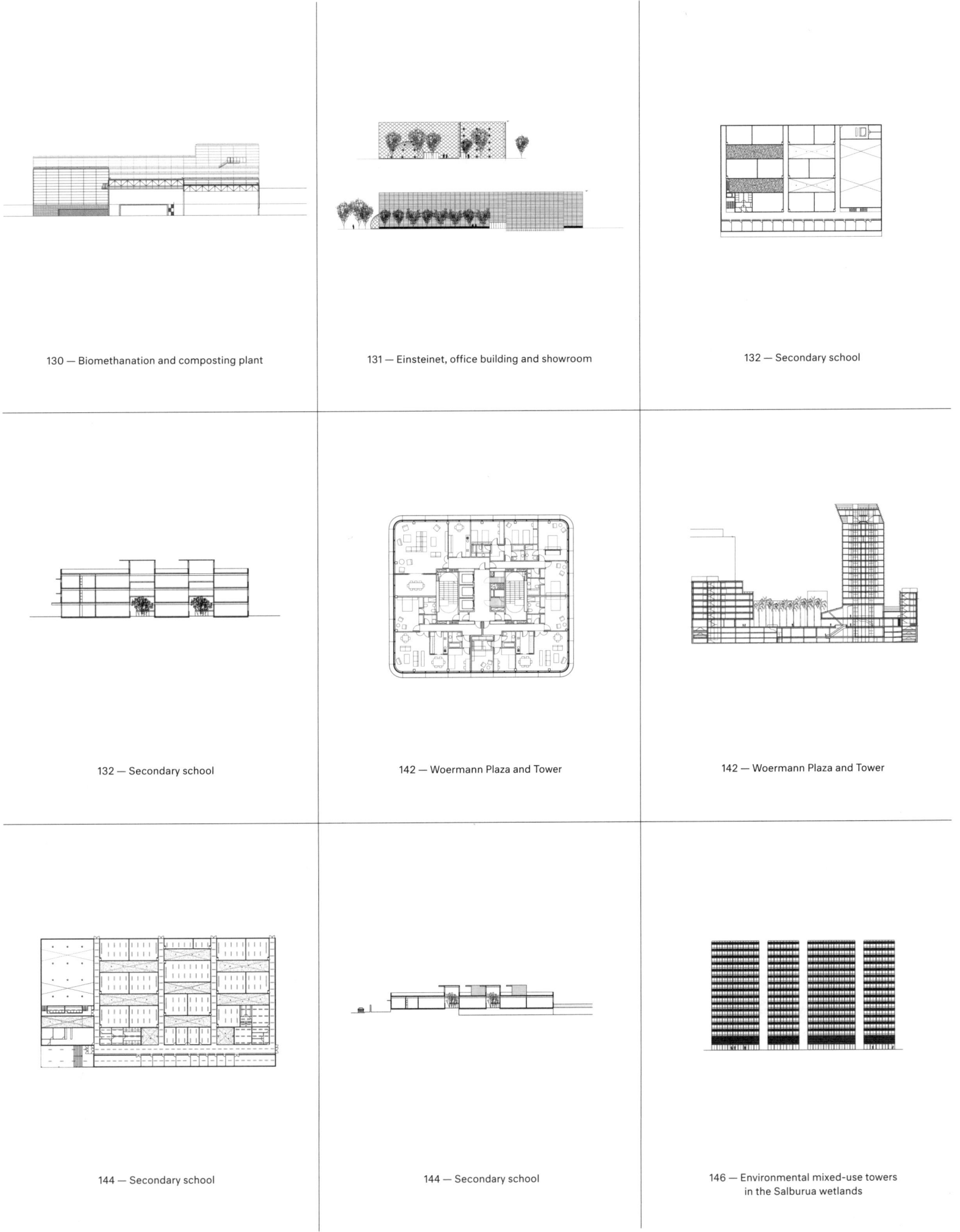

Kersten Geers and David Van Severen

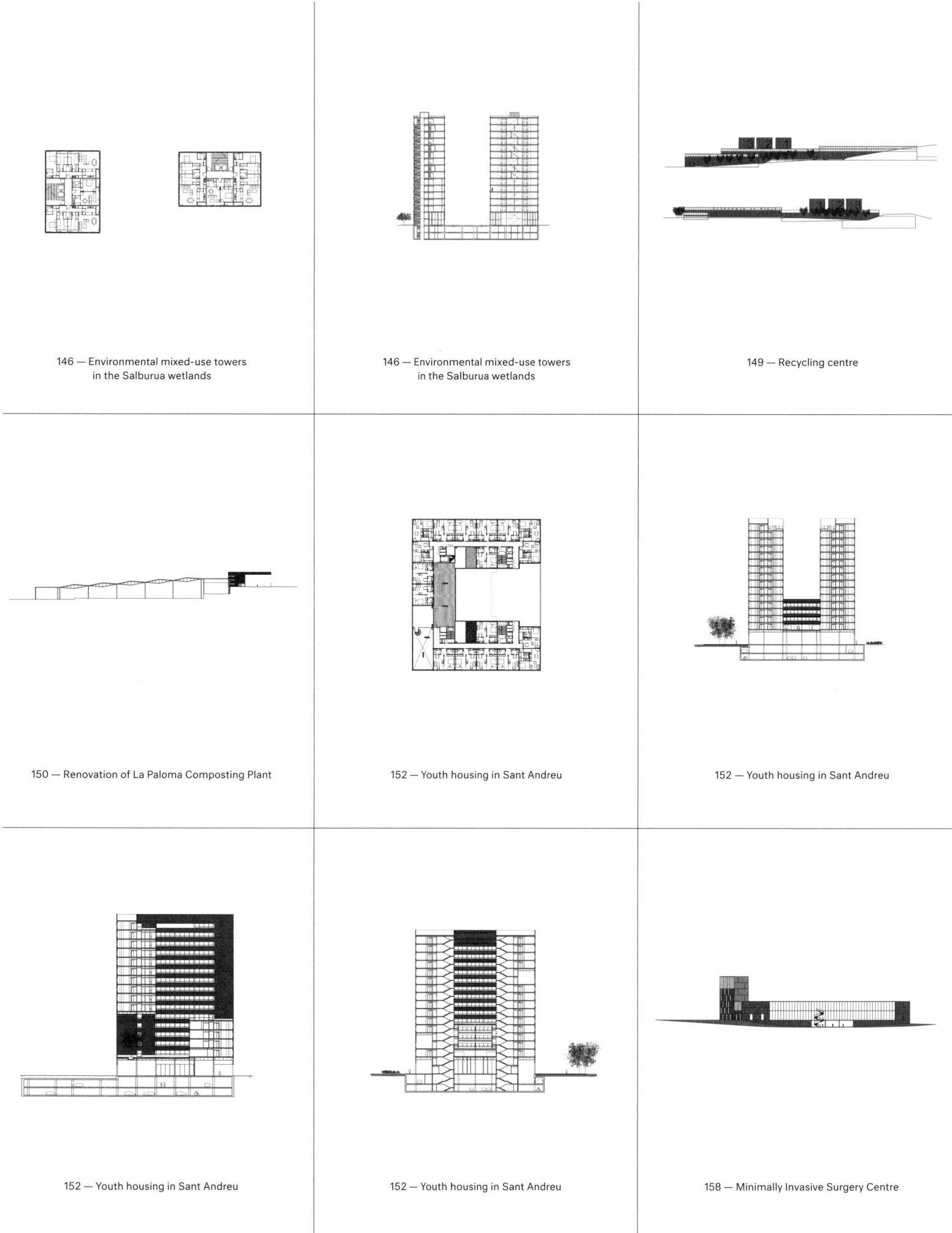

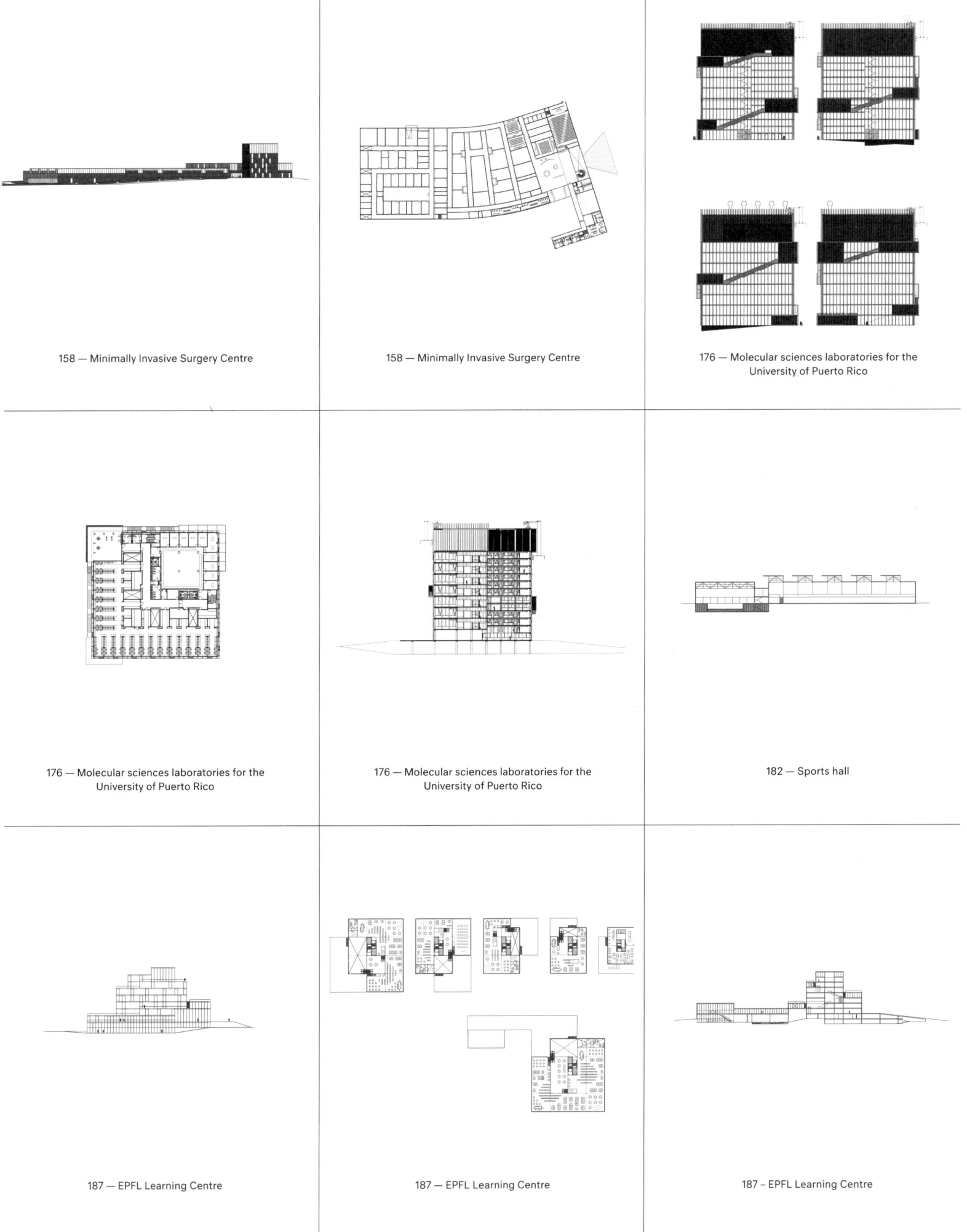

Kersten Geers and David Van Severen

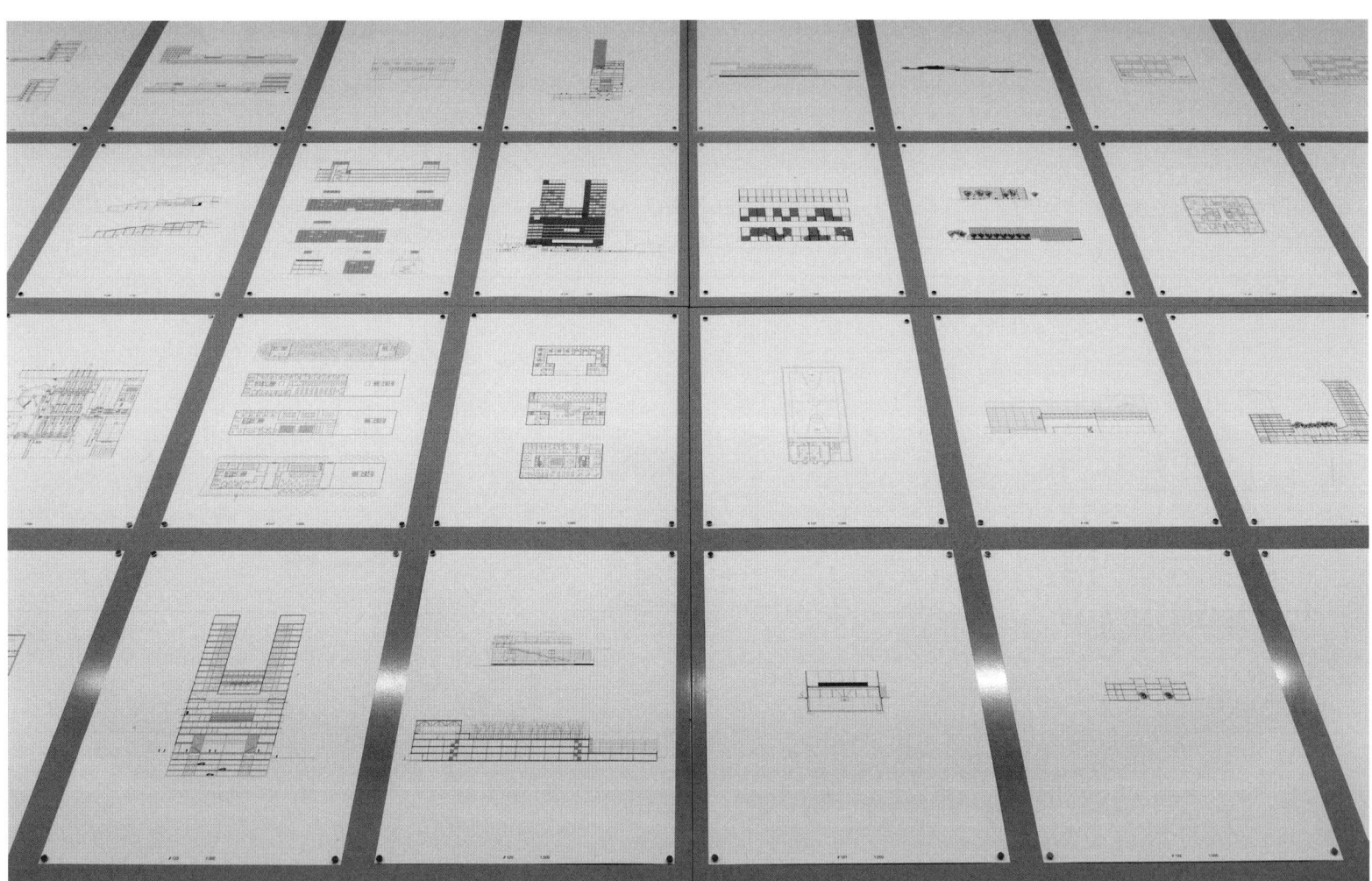

March 2015

Kersten Geers and David Van Severen unpack their research methodology and curatorial strategy. Comments by Iñaki Ábalos and Juan Herreros appear in red.

Kersten Geers: Our perspective relates to our own practice because we come from the practice of Ábalos & Herreros, in a way. We studied with Iñaki and Juan for only one year, but this experience was nevertheless important. As we looked through the material in the archive, it was as if we were tracing part of the lineage of our own work. The production we were dealing with became something like the meta-production of our own work.

The title of the exhibition, *Industrial Architecture*, refers perhaps most directly to three photographs by Lewis Baltz from a series which is part of the CCA collection: *The New Industrial Parks Near Irvine, California*. But *Industrial Architecture* also refers to a way of making the genealogy of buildings technically similar. The work of Ábalos & Herreros, operating at the outer edge of modernism, investigates machine-like logic and the endless multiplication of the system. Nothing is exactly original. Their work is always more an appropriation of an industrial idea of architecture rather than the creation of something entirely new.

David Van Severen: When we studied with Iñaki and Juan, in the late 1990s, we saw the work of Ábalos & Herreros at one of the most important moments for the office. During our research in the archive, we saw ourselves in the work, but we also saw differences. In addition to this experience of looking in a mirror, we found it interesting to position ourselves as mediators between the archive and the CCA as an archiving institution.

In the archive we discovered that the idea of the original was really not there, as Kersten was saying. In the 1990s, Ábalos & Herreros drew plans by hand but eventually they started using computers to produce iterations. The same is true of their collages, which were produced in AutoCAD after a certain point.

The material we encountered led us to ask how to show an archive without originals. We became interested in the idea of replicas and we made the blunt choice to show copies of the work in a series of printed AutoCAD drawings that represents an important part of their industrial, box-like architecture.

We also included photographs that show the materiality of the archive and that can apply to each of these plans, as well as a replica of a device that Ábalos & Herreros made for an installation in the 1990s. In our exhibition it shows references that we encountered as students.

KG: Showing reproductions of the work of an office that in our opinion was obsessed with reproductions, was at the core of what we wanted to do in the gallery. The drawings are all CAD drawings that were printed with careful assistance from the CCA. In a way it was a terrible job, because it is not just a matter of taking a drawing out of a paper file, framing it and hanging it. No, we had to find our way through a labyrinth of CAD universes and find out which was the final drawing (or maybe decide not to show the final drawing), print the drawing, choose line weights and with that set of decisions put the drawing on paper. We chose forty-two projects out of one hundred and fifty. But not all of the forty-two are proper projects; some of them are unfinished competitions.

• Even though we displayed the drawings in chronological order, it becomes clear that all of them are versions of each other. They are slight variations and family members rather than fundamentally new ideas. This could be understood as a problem but we thought of it as an excellent quality. In this series, one piece taken separately is irrelevant. But putting the pieces together makes something else entirely.

A second group of objects, as David mentioned, is a set of pictures of objects from the archive. We tried to stretch these objects as far as we could. There is a picture of a computer screen showing a rendering, an image which we found only in digital form. Stefano Graziani, whom we asked to take these pictures, photographed the computer screen directly. → P. 44

Another example is a folded sheet of A0 paper from the competition for the New Museum, for which Ábalos & Herreros were shortlisted. → P. 48

There is also a reference picture of a set of barns which we found in the project for a box-like building. The reference picture almost becomes the image of their project. This use of references was an important aspect of the way they worked, but it seems to us that it was also how they built up their universe.

With this in mind, we selected eighty teaching slides from their extensive

• Juan Herreros: The work of architects should not be approached as a collection of built projects. Actually Ábalos & Herreros had no more than twenty projects built. And fifteen or sixteen of them are less than 1,000 square metres. The built projects are the icebergs of our production, and everything in between is our body of work.

slide catalogue. Alongside the new technology of CAD was the old technology of taking slide pictures. Ábalos & Herreros did not take photographs so often but instead took rather rudimentary pictures of reference books. Slides show images of Gehry's parking garage in Santa Monica, Rossi's Centro Torri and César Pelli's Pacific Design Center, among many other projects. These are relatively blunt and direct references of the age. They are educational elements that, together with simple pictures that show projects like Breuer's Bijenkorf in Rotterdam, create enough visual material to allow the viewer to begin to understand the CAD drawings as projects. → Figs. 01–04

We did not intend to explain a specific project. A close look reveals that the printed CAD drawings are numbered. They have a scale and it is possible to understand where one project starts and another ends. But we wanted to show Ábalos & Herreros's body of work: their version of industrial architecture. Their work was a struggle but also a negotiation, almost like the negative of a picture plate that frames a reality as found. For that reason, Baltz is important. The reality as found in their world was a late-modern reality: partly Smithsons, partly Mies, partly shopping mall, and they produced an idea of an architecture that was an extreme echo of its time. They understood that the modernist project had been run to its absolute limit, and that the only way to show this was to employ the modernist strategy to the point at which it goes berserk.

DVS: Alejandro de la Sota's idea that architecture is not in the invention but in the intention was important for Ábalos & Herreros. Rather than original architecture, they made technical devices that hold a mirror to society. The exhibition's layout is in that sense important. We embraced the idea of showing the machine by making a replica of one of their installations. There are also the industrial tables that show the plans, the fluorescent tubes and the reproductions of what we found in the archive. Everything we found is heterogeneous and we framed it with homogeneous materialization in this space: the pictures, the plans, the slides and the reference pictures. For us, this is industrial architecture.

KG: Perhaps the archive of Ábalos & Herreros announces architecture archives of the future, more so than the archive of Álvaro Siza, for example, in which all drawings are kept. There is a kind of contemporary office like Ábalos & Herreros for which the problem of the original becomes a serious one. We were interested in exactly this: that the archive of an office that operated in the 1990s and later has hardly any physical material. What is the original in a production in which everything is drawn with AutoCAD and originals of collages are often digital?

In the case of Ábalos & Herreros's work, there are no originals. All the iterations before and after are relevant and to a certain extent also irrelevant. You can only show reproductions. You could even say that Lewis Baltz's pictures are only reproductions, albeit today extremely expensive ones.

01–04

Fig. 01: Marcel Breuer. De Bijenkorf department store, Rotterdam, 1955–1957. Colour slide, 5 × 5 cm. AP164.S3.D2.ARCH270816 / Fig. 02: Aldo Rossi. Centro Torri shopping centre, Parma, 1985–1988. Black-and-white slide, 5 × 5 cm. AP164.S3.D2.ARCH270838 / Fig. 03: Frank Gehry. Santa Monica Place, 1979–1981. Colour slide, 5 × 5 cm. AP164.S3.D2.ARCH270853 / Fig. 04: César Pelli. Pacific Design Center, Los Angeles, 1975. Colour slide, 5 × 5 cm. AP164.S3.D2.ARCH270854

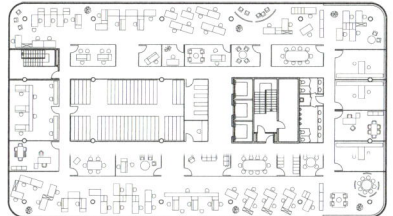 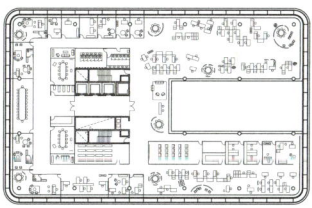 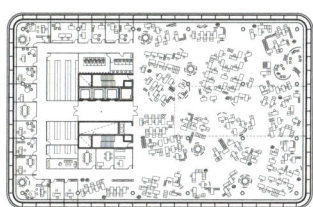 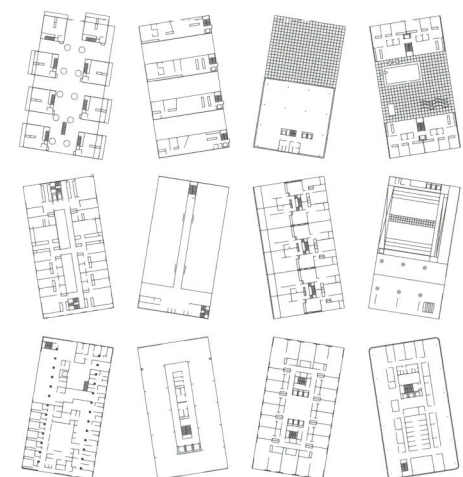

05–07

• JH: Our projects were driven by our theoretical work, but in a way these two activities were quite disparate. We did not write about the kind of projects we were working on. We wrote *Técnica y arquitectura* when we were teaching constructive systems in order to form a precise theory of the relationship between technics and architecture. The theoretical work is not a complement to the projects but is rather a laboratory of ideas. The movement from theory to project is not as direct as the reconfiguration of ideas from one project to the next.

You sometimes have to look very carefully to see that two CAD drawings correspond to two different projects. For example, project #83 seems to be a set of either #64 or #78. → Figs. 05–07

But #64 is a small office building that was actually built, whereas #78 was never built. The work is a set of relationships. It is clear from the AutoCAD files that quite often Ábalos&Herreros copied older files into new files, to make these groups of files. That is the way we used to draw in the 1990s, and the way we still do today sometimes.

Scale is an important topic. One plan at 1:250 and another at 1:500 almost look like the same plan. An image of a fax which was sent by Ábalos&Herreros to MIT Press, the publisher of the English translation of *Técnica y arquitectura en la ciudad contemporánea*, shows a handwritten comment that says that these two plans, which are reference images in the book, are not at the same scale. → P. 36

The publisher had to adjust the scales and look at the size of the tables in each plan to compare them.

•

In the gallery, noticing the different project numbers of the drawings and the difference in scale will help the viewer understand a lot.

DVS: Another set of drawings show Ábalos&Herreros's fascination with the technical skin: the building around these interiors. We categorized these files according to the project numbers that were in the computer and saw them as a series of industrial-architecture boxes. We knew the stories from people working in the office: everything was designed in AutoCAD. There was no other medium. As Kersten was saying, apart from line weights, we changed nothing about the drawings. But aside from the CAD files, we wanted to use photographs to show the hybrid material that we found in the archive.

We found some models, but they are almost coincidences in the office's production. One of Stefano's photographs of a Perspex model of a tower suggests a relationship with a poster they made for the New Museum competition in New York. We showed both the model and the poster as photographs because the idea of the original had no meaning for us. → P. 31

KG: However, these are original Stefano Graziani pictures. We indicated specifically to him which objects to photograph and that we also wanted context. For example, we told him that it is important to show the range of the IKEA prints. But Stefano is the author of these photographs, without question.

The PIRS environmental education centre is represented many different times. These are all versions of cut-out collages which became the reproduction used by Ábalos&Herreros. → P. 40

Fig. 05: Plan of an administrative building for the Ministry of the Interior, Madrid, 1990–1992. AutoCAD drawing. AP164.S1.1990.D3 /
Fig. 06: Plans of the head office of the Savings Bank of Granada, 1992. AutoCAD drawing. AP164.S1.1992.D4 / Fig. 07: Planning proposal for the Abandoibarra area, Bilbao, 1993. AutoCAD drawing. AP164.S1.1993.D5

By comparing it to other elements, you see a narrative of how a family is made. That is how we wanted it to work: every illustration works for every plan, every plan for every slide and every slide for every picture.

DVS: It was crucial not to make a selection of archival material but rather to discover things and try to categorize them. It was a struggle, but the CAD files helped a lot. We made categories on the wall of our working space with the shape of the file we remembered, and numbered them. Then we looked through the archive to see what was in the folder of that project, whether printed or digital. There is no direct relation between one project and another: it is the ensemble that provides a view of their work.

KG: You could call the CAD drawings false friends. *Éventuellement* in French and *eventually* in English mean very different things, but look like friends. False friends became an important guiding principle as we made the selection. This drawing looks like that one, which looks like that one, but actually that is not true because one is at a different scale or in a different material. This relationship resonates with our own production as well. When you look at the details, you see a specific building. But if you look at the general idea of the building, you start to find some *faux amis*, like this building with the double tower. This complex building, in which a tower is stuck onto a box, which is stuck onto a big hall, appears over and over again in this set of false friends. → Figs. 08–10

Each version reflects on the construction system: the column, the beam, the floor. The scales of these buildings are different and plans become simpler, more rigid and maybe even less specific across the set. The same is true for the plan of the Woermann Tower. → Fig. 11

The section is quite distinct, but if you look again at #64 and #78, you see this false-friends relationship. And Sáenz de Oiza is important for that set.

DVS: The idea of false friends is very close to the relationship between original and reproduction. During the period we are concerned with—the 1990s and the early 2000s—the problem of the archive and the original was already present in the work of Ábalos & Herreros. And so the title *Industrial Architecture* could also be not original.

KG: We could have grouped all the sets of false friends together. But we felt that would have been reductive because the interesting point is that one plan or one section could be a building in its own right, and if we organized the plans into groups, part of that narrative would disappear. The work is interesting because it has cross-references.

The truth is that there are probably no more than four, five or six main formal ideas in the work. For example, there is the box with the boxes on top. This is a typical industrial building, but Ábalos & Herreros emphasize the form. It is possible to make a connection between the projects presented chronologically, and by taking out all the projects that do not fit the argument, we strengthened the argument.

Ábalos & Herreros drew from the work of the Smithsons, Charles and Ray Eames, Mies and De la Sota.

•

This work is important to our own practice, too. Our work has other influences, such as Ungers and Rossi,

• **JH: We often misinterpret *global* to mean *international*. Oiza and De la Sota were not international architects, but they had a sophisticated, global way of thinking. The contemporary project is to choose things and put them together. Today, because of the Internet, every architect in the world has the same information. Access to information is not a means of selection.**

08–10

Fig. 08: Section of *El Mirador*: mixed-used tower on the Bay of Gibraltar, Algeciras, 1999. AutoCAD drawing. AP164.S1.1999.D10 / Fig. 09: Section of one of the environmental mixed-use towers in the Salburua wetlands, Vitoria-Gasteiz, 2002–2006. AutoCAD drawing. AP164.S1.2002.D2 / Fig. 10: Section of a project for youth housing in Sant Andreu, Barcelona, 2002. AutoCAD drawing. AP164.S1.2002.D8

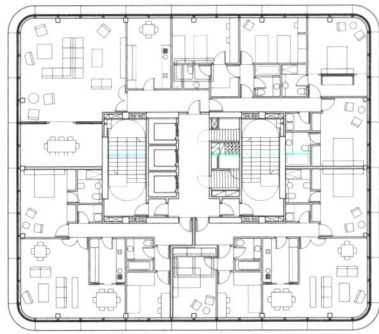

11

•• Iñaki Ábalos: Composition was quite important in all the projects. Although the projects look very dry, the proportions of objects obsessed us. It was as if we were making Doric temples.

To what extent is our way of using references alive, and to what extent has it been overtaken by new catalogues or manuals like *ArchDaily* and *Dezeen*, that show one million images in one minute? Is there a way to use these parameters to construct an identity?

••• IA: I have never discussed this with Juan, but I think we were creating an image. We were supposedly part of a style that *El Croquis* was spreading through Spanish architecture, but I do not agree with this.

in particular *Architecture of the City*. This was never part of the work of Ábalos&Herreros—or so we thought until we found some slide pictures of Rossi buildings in the archive. Their references were apparently slightly wider than the way we experienced them.

Their idea of the envelope, the perimeter, is something that we carried with us subconsciously, although our attitude is not necessarily the way they would have approached the perimeter. A large part of the work of Ábalos&Herreros negotiates with landscape architecture and addresses transformations of landscape, but we chose to exclude this work from our selection. For example, the recycling plant is part of a landscape plan, but if the landscape part is represented then the narrative that interests us becomes clouded. → Fig. 12

We focused instead on perimeters of buildings because that is a concern for us in our own practice.

DVS: Ábalos&Herreros's industrial architecture is related to our interest in an economy of means. Their way of working and their use of references show that a project does not need to be fancy. It can be quite dry and industrial, but it is never generic. This is something that inspired us in Madrid and that we apply today in our practice.

••

KG: The discourse of Ábalos&Herreros on an economy of means is concerned with the industrial catalogue, whereas our interest is more in the construction of the possible argument of the economy of means than it is about the catalogue. Our work might sometimes resemble the catalogue, but it never is. It is more indebted to classicism and Mies. Something looks straight but in fact it is not built straight; perception is much more important for us than it is for them.

When we studied with Iñaki and Juan, their focus was moving toward what they called the natural artificial. This concept addresses both the landscape and the building. It is evident in these buildings that have strange proportions or that stand in a particular way on the site, like the gymnastics pavilion in Retiro Park, which is half underground. Ábalos&Herreros were obsessed with the natural, but they built artificial structures rather than trying to mimic the natural.

They drew from Le Corbusier and from Mies to a certain extent, but also simply from the rudimentary technology of Spanish architecture at the time. They should be placed in the context of Rafael Moneo's poetic regionalism, a context which they entered almost as engineers. They tried to reclaim an idea of engineering as architecture, and the resulting architecture is ugly. Their architecture has a 1980s negotiation with corrugated steel and mirror glass, but it is very nasty.

•••

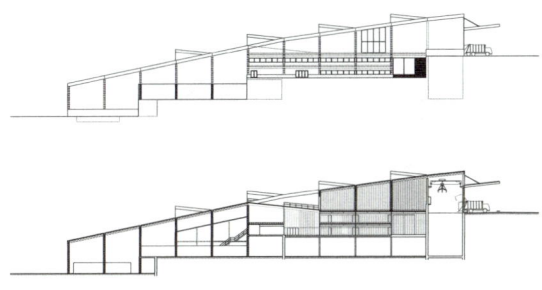

12

Fig. 11: Plan of the Woermann Tower, Las Palmas de Gran Canaria, 2001–2005. AutoCAD drawing. AP164.S1.2001.D7 / Fig. 12: Section of the recycling plant for urban waste, Valdemingómez, Madrid, 1996–1999. AutoCAD drawing. AP164.S1.1996.D4

13

• JH: We had many references, and not all of them came from the world of architecture. We had an extensive collection of images that came from very different fields, from art to publicity and science. In the case of the double tower, our reference was a mix between the cathedral of Notre-Dame de Paris and the Dakota Building in New York.

DVS: In order to present the reference material, we made a replica of the slide projector that Ábalos&Herreros designed for the Third Biennial of Spanish Architecture and Urbanism in 1996 and 1997. → Fig. 13

In the collection of slides, we found many references that they showed us during our studies. References to art, including works by David Hockney and Ed Ruscha, are present alongside architecture. This slide projector introduces their teaching into the exhibition and shows their view of architecture as a set of principles of structure, of facade and of climatic devices.

•

KG: Slides include work by Charles and Ray Eames and of the BEST Products Showroom by Venturi, Rauch and Scott Brown. The combination is close to insanity. → Figs. 14–15

The shopping mall and Le Corbusier are both present. Ábalos&Herreros made this device to display Spanish architecture. They insisted that the only way to do this was through pictures. They made a few of these objects and installed them in the space, standing on a Gerhard Richter carpet. We thought the CCA's gallery was an appropriate place to reproduce this object. It always had two projectors, and this double projection melds the narratives.

DVS: The work of Ábalos&Herreros cannot survive without these references. It was important to bring the references into this space, to show the many layers of the work.

KG: Another slide shows a drawing by Alejandro de la Sota that could be a drawing of one of the projects represented on the table. But it is indeed De la Sota, whose work they copied throughout their career. → Fig. 16

Ábalos&Herreros began as teachers of construction. They carved out a position by embracing De la Sota in a new way. Everyone was a fan of Alejandro de la Sota, but Ábalos&Herreros saw him as Mies, reinterpreted: a kind of Aldi Mies, the cheap version. From this position, through commercial architecture, they built up a counter-narrative. Not many people understood them in this early period, but in a very short while they gathered a group of people around them, including Eduardo Arroyo and Federico Soriano. Ábalos&Herreros were

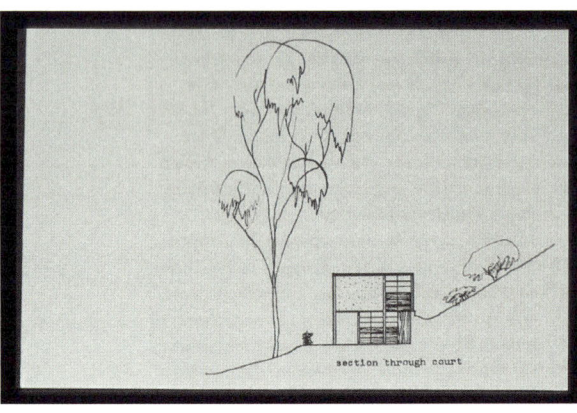 

14–15

Fig. 13: Photograph of an installation in Madrid in 1997, designed by Ábalos& Herreros for the Third Biennial of Spanish Architecture and Urbanism, showing the viewing device. Gelatin silver print, 17.7 × 23.8 cm. AP164. S1.1995.D2.ARCH276950 / Fig. 14: Charles and Ray Eames. Case Study House no. 8, Pacific Palisades, California, 1945–1949. Black-and-white slide, 5 × 5 cm. AP164.S3.D2.ARCH270824 / Fig. 15: Robert Venturi, John Rauch and Denise Scott Brown. BEST Products Showroom, Langhorne, Pennsylvania, 1973–1979. Colour slide, 5 × 5 cm. AP164.S3.D2.ARCH270852

16

very much the counter-revolution: the non-materialists and enthusiasts of Renzo Piano. They liked all the wrong people and they did not get their *Croquis* monograph, which was very important in Spain at that time.

We had some disappointment during this research. Sometimes we thought that we would find three hundred beautiful documents related to a project, and we did not even find one. At other times we made a discovery, which we then questioned. We debated whether the IKEA is a good or bad project. We didn't know this project beforehand. Is there an interesting connection to Ed Ruscha and America? Or is it a complete projection on our part to think that a banal IKEA is more than just a banal IKEA. Ultimately, isn't every IKEA just a blue box with the word *IKEA* on it? → P. 50

DVS: We had an idealized image of what we studied, which led to disappointment. Over the course of this research we discovered that what we remember from our studies had transformed and had become the concerns of our own current practice. But perhaps this was also our task: to keep this idealized world alive through this exercise with the archive.

KG: It is indeed an idealization, as pragmatic as it might appear. But the pressure of presenting an objective account of the archive—to the extent that this is possible—fell away for us because we knew that two other readings of this archive were immediately forthcoming. We were not afraid to make formalist decisions. We connected a sequence of plans to a sequence of slides and to a sequence of photographs of fragments of material in order to construct a possible oeuvre of Ábalos & Herreros.

Fig. 16: Alejandro de la Sota. Housing development, Alcúdia, Mallorca, 1983–1984. Black-and-white slide, 5 × 5 cm. AP164.S3.D2.ARCH270821

October 2014

Juan José Castellón González discusses objects he encounters during his research residency in the Ábalos & Herreros archive.

Juan José Castellón González

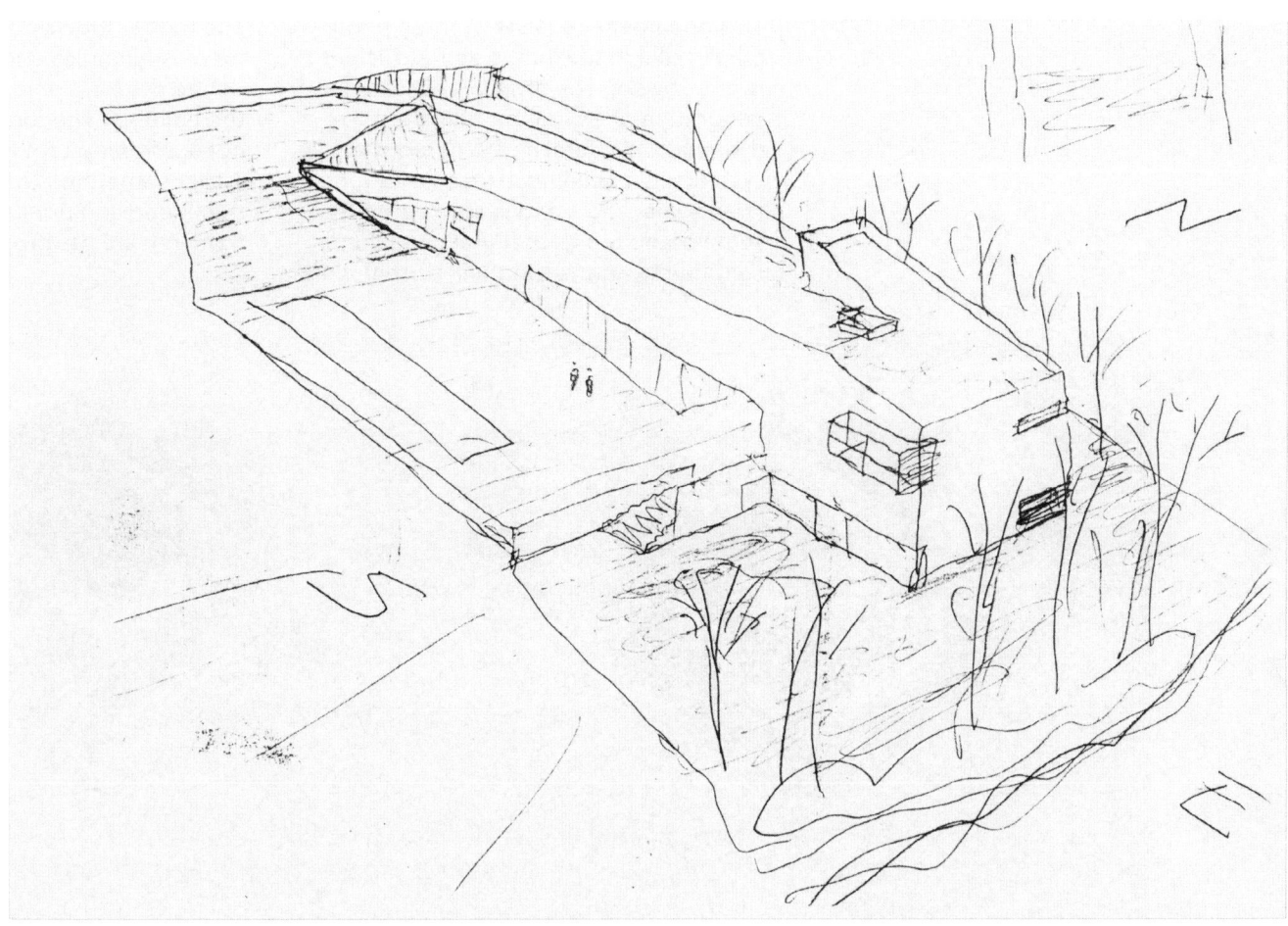

Juan José Castellón González: The drawing of Casa Verde, and the project as a whole, express the duality of the natural and the artificial, or how the building and nature are merged into one system. The project positions conventional systems in an unconventional context. The technique of this sketch shows a perspectival approach and the construction of a vectorial space, which was one of Ábalos&Herreros's concerns. The result is a perception of the project that corresponds to the viewer's experience of approaching the building. The technique of representation therefore supports the logic that underpins the drawing: a hybrid of the building and nature.

The landscape becomes the building: the slope becomes the ramp and the ramp becomes the roof, and in one gesture nature and building are merged. The building's skin shows this transformation as well; from a natural landscape, it becomes an artificial facade and a conventional technical system. For the facade, Ábalos&Herreros used a checker block, which is a component that is often used for parking garages that include some grass at the top.

Above: Sketch of Casa Verde, 1997. Electrophotographic print, 29.7 × 42 cm.
AP164.S1.1997.D4.ARCH275369

Juan José Castellón González

This document consists of three photographs of a model of the self-sufficient hybrid towers. The project addresses the integration of environmental, thermodynamic, structural and programmatic systems in a building. It was developed twenty years ago, and is connected to some of the topics that Iñaki and Juan continue to address in their current work.

The model shows how program, thermodynamics and technical solutions define the form and the structure of the building. The form is a consequence: not something that is imposed but rather something that is generated by the underlying principles and systems that activate the project.

This is a collage of the AH-Gia Houses, which is one of my favourite Ábalos&Herreros projects. The project expresses not just the duality of the magical box and the technical artifact, but also a playful attitude in the face of the complexity that is inherent in the project. Ábalos&Herreros bring playfulness even to dry and technical work. The plans for this project are extremely technical, and the project is based on the combination of standard systems. But behind this technical solution is a theory of a new approach to housing.

The document is a collage, and in a way it is a materialization of the lightness in the work of Ábalos& Herreros. This attitude can be related to art and to pop, but also to an approach to things that are beyond the architect's control. This approach gives the freedom to react to complex situations unconventionally and lightly. The technique of collage is closely related to the way Ábalos&Herreros worked, in the design process as well as onsite. They gathered different systems, different techniques and different theories and combined them in a single project.

Opposite: Photographic sequence of a study model showing the program and structure of the Zephyr Competition self-sufficient hybrid towers, 1994. Chromogenic colour prints, 8.1 × 21 cm.
AP164.S1.1994.D2.ARCH271736,
AP164.S1.1994.D2.ARCH271737,
AP164.S1.1994.D2.ARCH271735

Above: Collage for the industrialized housing prototypes: AH-Gia Houses, c. 1993–1996. Chromogenic colour prints and paper, 23 × 42.8 cm.
AP164.S1.1993.D11.ARCH273427

Juan José Castellón González develops his research in the exhibition *Jai Tech.*

Ábalos&Herreros
selected by

Juan José
Castellón González

24 May–12 July
2015

Jai Tech

Jai Tech
Material included in the exhibition

Iñaki Ábalos and Juan Herreros on the roof
of the cathedral of Notre-Dame de Paris, c. 1990
Electrostatic print
AP164.S2.SS2.ARCH270446

#091

Concurso Zephyr : torres mixtas autosuficientes
Zephyr Competition : self-sufficient hybrid towers, Madrid, 1994

AP164.S1.1994.D2

View of a study model showing building facades and structure
Chromogenic colour print
AP164.S1.1994.D2.ARCH271740

#142

Plaza y torre Woermann
Woermann Plaza and Tower, Las Palmas de Gran Canaria,
2001–2005

AP164.S1.2001.D7

View of a site model showing the plaza and tower in the urban context
AP164.S1.2001.D7.ARCH269001

#146

Torres mixtas bioclimáticas en el Humedal de Salburua
Environmental mixed-use towers in the Salburua wetlands, Vitoria-Gasteiz, 2002–2006
AP164.S1.2002.D2

View of a site model showing the four towers and surrounding wetlands
AP164.S1.2002.D2.ARCH269172

Contextual Strategy: Topological Gestures
– Should we twist it or rotate it?

#091   Cut-out views of a model showing site context, building facades and structure
Gelatin silver prints
AP164.S1.1994.D2.ARCH271732, AP164.S1.1994.D2.ARCH271733

#142   Rendering of the plaza and tower in the urban context
Ink-jet print
AP164.S1.2001.D7.ARCH271726

#142   Rendering of the plaza and tower
Ink-jet print
AP164.S1.2001.D7.ARCH271725

#091   Mock-up for a presentation panel showing context maps, plans and views
Collage of electrostatic prints on translucent paper, black ink and tape, on drafting film
AP164.S1.1994.D2.ARCH271746

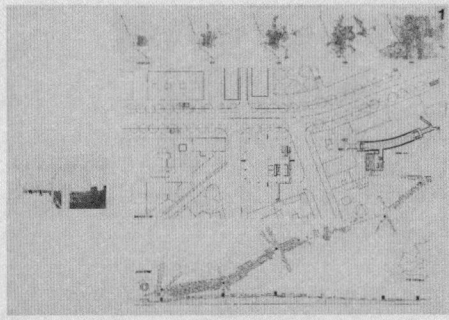

#146   Site, parking and access floor plans
Electrostatic print
AP164.S1.2002.D2.ARCH271750:053

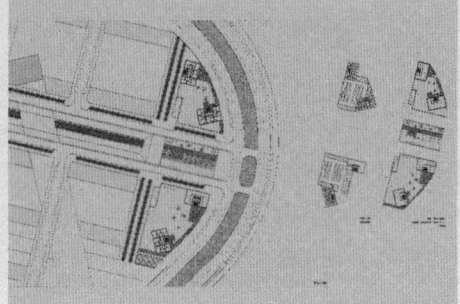

#146   Site plan showing the urban context and Salburua Park, a wetland habitat
Electrostatic print
AP164.S1.2002.D2.ARCH271750:055

#146   Context map showing the site in relation to the historic centre of Vitoria-Gasteiz and Salburua Park
Electrostatic print
AP164.S1.2002.D2.ARCH271750:057

#142   Ground-floor plan showing artist Albert Oehlen's paving design for the plaza
Ink-jet print
AP164.S1.2001.D7.ARCH272006

#146   Construction views showing the access road and surrounding wetlands
Ink-jet print
AP164.S1.2002.D2.ARCH271750:049

#142   Views showing the beachfront and isthmus of Las Palmas de Gran Canaria, and sketches of the design
Ink-jet print
AP164.S1.2001.D7.ARCH272021

#091   Mock-up for a presentation panel describing the aim, site plan, problems and resolutions of the project
Collage of electrostatic prints and tape on translucent paper
AP164.S1.1994.D2.ARCH271742

#146   Photomontage of a panoramic view from a tower
Exhibition print
AP164.S1.2002.D2.ARCH276125

#142   Site model
Fibreboard, printed paper, plastic, cardboard, paint and wood
AP164.S1.2001.D7.ARCH269001

#146   Site model
Wood, plastic and grey paint
AP164.S1.2002.D2.ARCH269172

II Programmatic Strategy: Hybrid Organizations
– Why don't we put the city inside it?

091   Photographic sequence of a study model showing the program and structure
Chromogenic colour prints
AP164.S1.1994.D2.ARCH271736, AP164.S1.1994.D2.ARCH271737, AP164.S1.1994.D2.ARCH271735

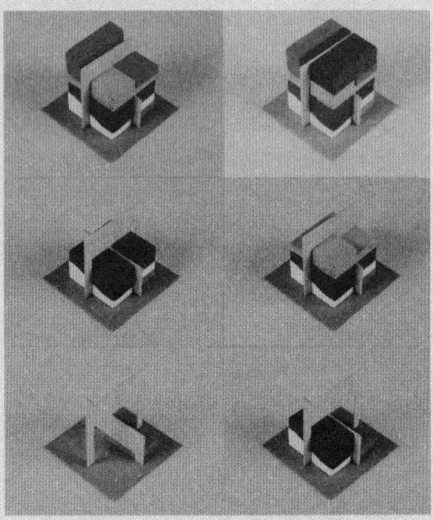

146   Section of a tower and diagrammatic studies calculating the program layout and area
Scale 1:375 (section)
Digital print
AP164.S1.2002.D2.ARCH271716

142   Longitudinal section of plaza and tower showing program layout
Scale 1:300
Ink-jet print
AP164.S1.2001.D7.ARCH272005

142   Plans of the plaza and tower showing typical office and residential floors
Scale 1:300
Ink-jet print
AP164.S1.2001.D7.ARCH272316

091   Mock-up for a presentation panel showing sections of a tower and the program layout
Collage of electrostatic prints, printed number and tape on translucent paper
AP164.S1.1994.D2.ARCH271747

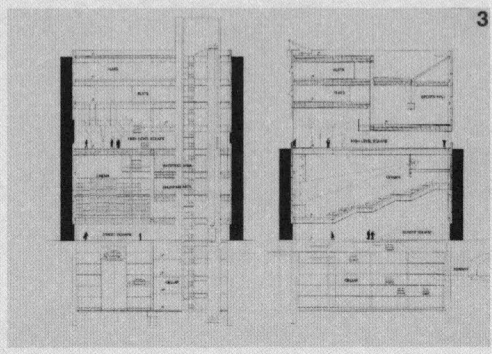

146   Partial plans of a tower showing various living unit typologies
Digital print
AP164.S1.2002.D2.ARCH271718

146   Floor plans of the four towers showing living units, offices and ground-floor retail space
Ink-jet print
AP164.S1.2002.D2.ARCH272319

142   Rooftop and floor-plan typologies
Scale 1:200
Ink-jet print
AP164.S1.2001.D7.ARCH271712

091   Mock-up for a presentation panel showing floor plans
Collage of electrostatic prints, black ink and tape on translucent paper
AP164.S1.1994.D2.ARCH272316

III Structural Strategy: Constructional Systems
– How do we assemble it?

#091   Mock-up for a presentation panel showing facade elevations, axonometric views of a structural frame and furniture wall and a section detail of a living unit
Collage of electrostatic prints, drafting appliqué, pen and ink, graphite, printed number and tape on translucent paper and drafting film
AP164.S1.1994.D2.ARCH271745

#142   Section detail of living units in the tower
Original scale 1:20, print scale 1:40
Exhibition print
AP164.S1.2001.D7.ARCH277006

#091   Page from a presentation booklet showing various structural details
Electrostatic print
AP164.S1.1994.D2.ARCH270892:003

#146   Construction views
Laser prints
AP164.S1.2002.D2.ARCH271887:010, AP164.S1.2002.D2.ARCH271887:011

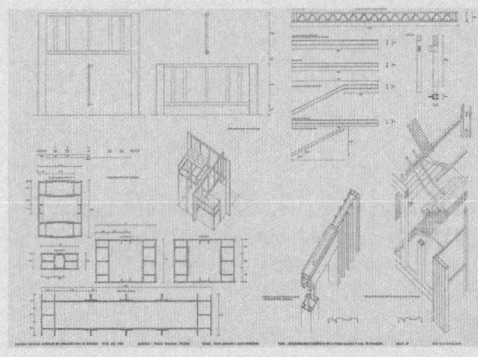

#142   Photomontaged view of the project nearing completion
Chromogenic colour prints
AP164.S1.2001.D7.ARCH271720

#091   Page from a presentation booklet showing a section detail of a living unit
Electrostatic print
AP164.S1.1994.D2.ARCH270892:013

#146   Section details of living units, facades and the roof
Scale 1:30 and 1:10
Ink-jet print
AP164.S1.2002.D2.ARCH272007

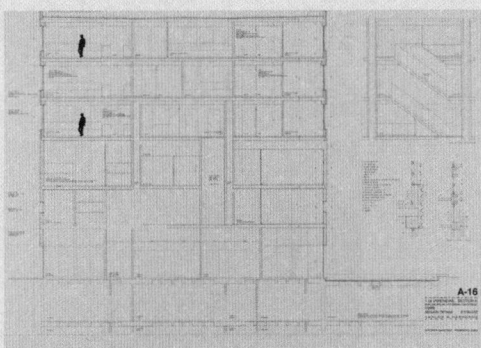

#146   Construction views showing the surrounding wetlands
Ink-jet print with notations in graphite, pen and ink
AP164.S1.2002.D2.ARCH271750:047

|||| Thermodynamic Strategy: Self-Sufficient Buildings
— *Should we call it science or common sense?*

#091   Mock-up for a presentation panel describing the climatic properties of the roof structures of the sports hall and shopping area in winter and summer
Collage of electrostatic prints, black ink and tape on translucent paper
AP164.S1.1994.D2.ARCH271741

#091   Mock-up for a presentation panel describing the ventilation system of the windows in the living units and the air-conditioning system throughout the tower
Collage of electrostatic print and tape on translucent paper
AP164.S1.1994.D2.ARCH271744

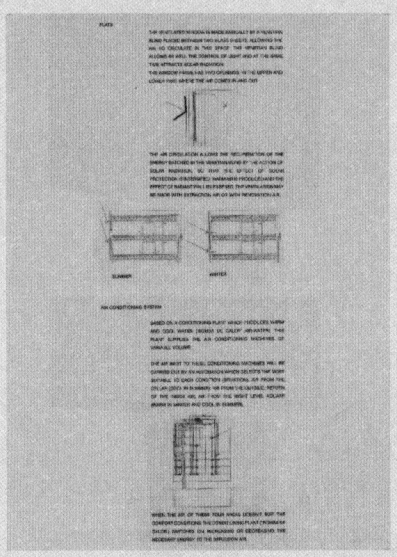

#091   Mock-up for a presentation panel describing the bioclimatic strategy of the tower facades in winter and summer
Collage of electrostatic prints and tape on translucent paper
AP164.S1.1994.D2.ARCH271743

#142   Page layout showing facade details of brise-soleil and thickened glass, and an interior view of the tower
Ink-jet print
AP164.S1.2001.D7.ARCH271724

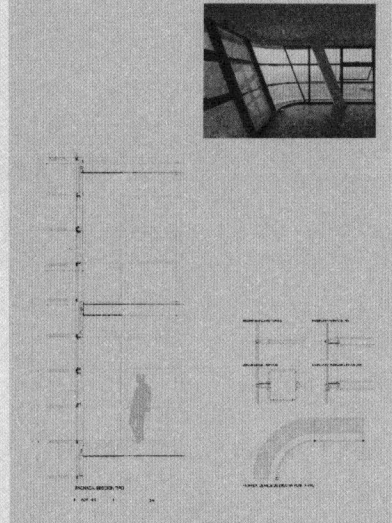

#146   Diagrams of tower shadows and energy-harnessing areas
Digital print
AP164.S1.2002.D2.ARCH271719

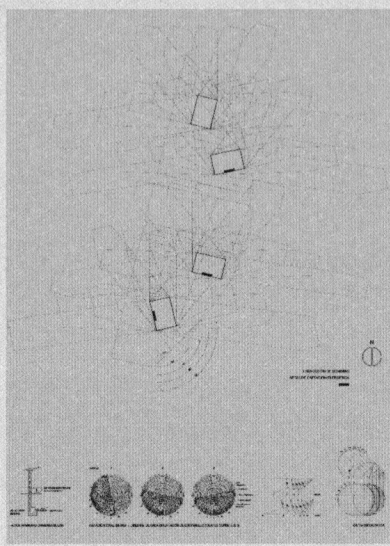

#146   Sketch of an interior view of a tower with annotations stating, *"What is important here is what is not seen: modules, machinery, technical ceilings, etc."*
Exhibition print
AP164.S1.2002.D2.ARCH276126

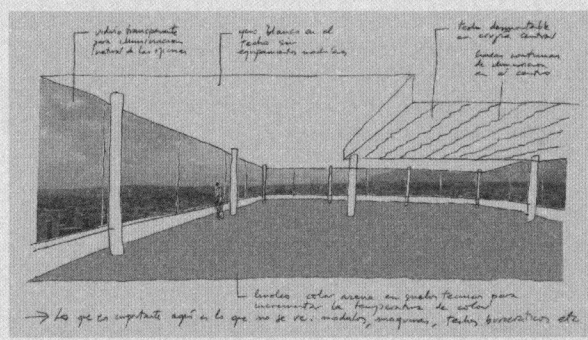

 Superficial Strategy: Fragile Skins
— What should it wear today?

#146 Facade details with bioclimatic diagrams
Digital print
AP164.S1.2002.D2.ARCH271717

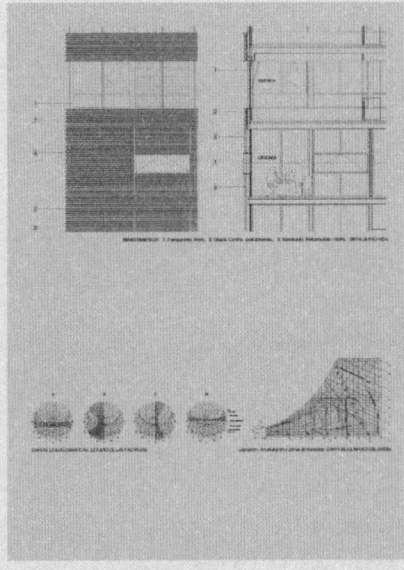

#146 Facade details showing cladding and fenestration of the apartment and retail units
Digital print
AP164.S1.2002.D2.ARCH271750:054

#091 Page from a presentation booklet showing elevations, structural details and model views of the facades
Electrostatic print
AP164.S1.1994.D2.ARCH270892:004

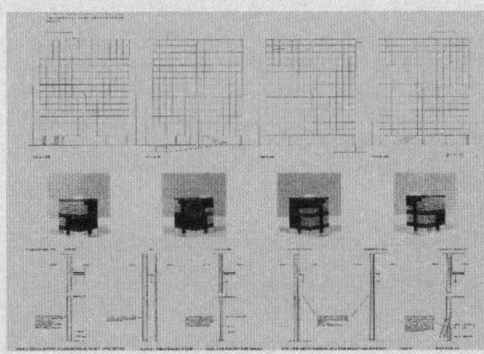

#091 View of a model
Chromogenic colour print
AP164.S1.1994.D2.ARCH271740

#142 View of the tower showing operable windows, brise-soleil and plant-motif windows
Ink-jet print
AP164.S1.2001.D7.ARCH272154

#142 Page layout showing floor plans, section and partial views of the tower
Ink-jet print
AP164.S1.2001.D7.ARCH271723

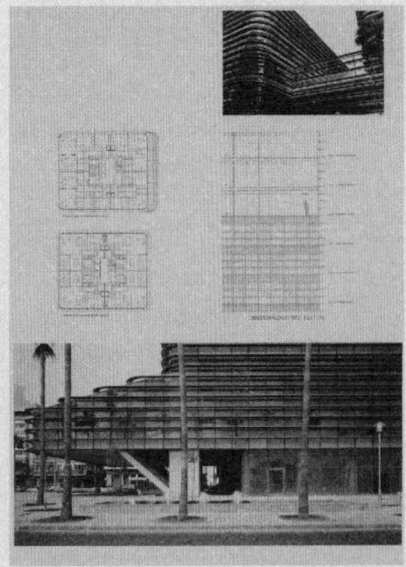

#142 View of custom windows showing plant motifs
Exhibition print
AP164.S1.2001.D7.ARCH277008

#142 View looking through a plant-motif window
Exhibition print
AP164.S1.2001.D7.ARCH277010

#146 View of coloured spray-foam insulation, to be seen through translucent polycarbonate panels
Exhibition print
AP164.S1.2002.D2.ARCH276127

#142 Studies of plant motifs for windows
Ink-jet prints
AP164.S1.2001.D7.ARCH272010, AP164.S1.2001.D7.ARCH272011,
AP164.S1.2001.D7.ARCH272013, AP164.S1.2001.D7.ARCH272014,
AP164.S1.2001.D7.ARCH272015, AP164.S1.2001.D7.ARCH272016

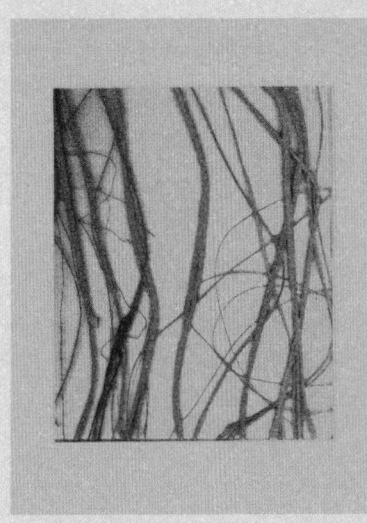

Jai tech | From the Basque *jai*: festivity, and the English *tech*: technology. sb. | Construction process, projectural definition or technical experimentation founded on facility, laughter, subjectivity, collage and the market. *Jai-tech* considers that the definition of an architectonic object cannot emerge through suffering, from the epic or heroic, and neither from modern or clichéd readings of mechanicity. Above all it defends the use of the latest technical advances for their potential to pervert or propose spatial organisation, in jettisoning purely figurative or narrative qualities. It takes a highly confrontational stance towards both contemporary *High Tech* and the currents defended by the official academy. Among its characteristics we may discern the use of catalogues, a tendency to resolve problems with minimal resources, the gin and tonic, the disappearance of the program in the definition of architectonic form, the sparing use of struts. Instead of stainless steel, galvanized steel. Instead of drag and merge, scissors and paste. Instead of a typology derived from industrial imagery, the consequential typology of energetic isotropy.

Being a way of thinking not strictly delimited by the material condition of building, its application to other disciplines, including theoretical or critical ones, such as urbanism, philosophy or music, is being investigated at the time this definition has been worded.

Iñaki Ábalos and Juan Herreros, Áreas de impunidad | Areas of Impunity
(Barcelona: Actar, 1997), 91–92.

Ábalos&Herreros office playlist
circa 2003–2006

Super Furry Animals

Hello Sunshine

3:40, 2003

Super Furry Animals

Golden Retriever

2:26, 2003

Starsailor

Silence is Easy

3:40, 2003

Los Piratas

Años 80

3:41, 2001

Los Piratas

El Equilibrio es Imposible

3:20, 2001

El Cuarteto de Nos

Nada es Gratis en la Vida

3:48, 2006

The Jayhawks

Save it for a Rainy Day

3:08, 2003

Maga

Agosto Esquimal

4:01, 2002

Fangoria

Retorciendo Palabras

3:58, 2004

Kiko Veneno

Echo de Menos

4:18, 1992

Jai Tech
Juan José Castellón González

Light construction is a concept that, in the field of architecture, is commonly associated with the heroic aspiration of constructing buildings without weight so that they almost disappear. Considering the high-rise building as a battlefield, this aspiration becomes a fight against gravity and materiality, which is in a certain sense a fight against existence. In this struggle, architects are equipped with high-tech weapons such as glass that changes in opacity, LED facades that collect and emit information, wind turbines, photovoltaic cells and ultralight materials. And of course all of these devices have proper certificates of energy efficiency and sustainability.

However, light construction has another meaning: one in which lightness is not just a physical quality, but an attitude. Lightness becomes a game of intelligence rather than a fight against complexity. Here, the high-rise building becomes a laboratory and the mixed-use program a catalyst for design strategies. Nourished by traditional and contemporary building techniques and by strategic architectural thinking, the methods of this light construction are at a distance from the vast resources of the high tech. This is the *jai tech*.* It is what we could define as common sense in architecture. It is about working with minimal resources and maximal architectural ambition, but also about the acceptance of imperfection and the Dionysian joy of existence. This interest in lightness was built and nurtured by masters of Spanish architecture such as Alejandro de la Sota, Francisco Javier Sáenz de Oiza, Miguel Fisac, Josep Lluís Sert and José Antonio Coderch. This is a lineage of architects to which Ábalos&Herreros are legitimate heirs, and a lineage that today is extended by a generation of architects who learned from them in turn.

*This term is derived from the Basque *jai*: festivity, and the English *tech*: technology. It originally appears in Iñaki Ábalos and Juan Herreros, *Áreas de impunidad* | *Areas of Impunity* (Barcelona: Actar, 1997), 91.

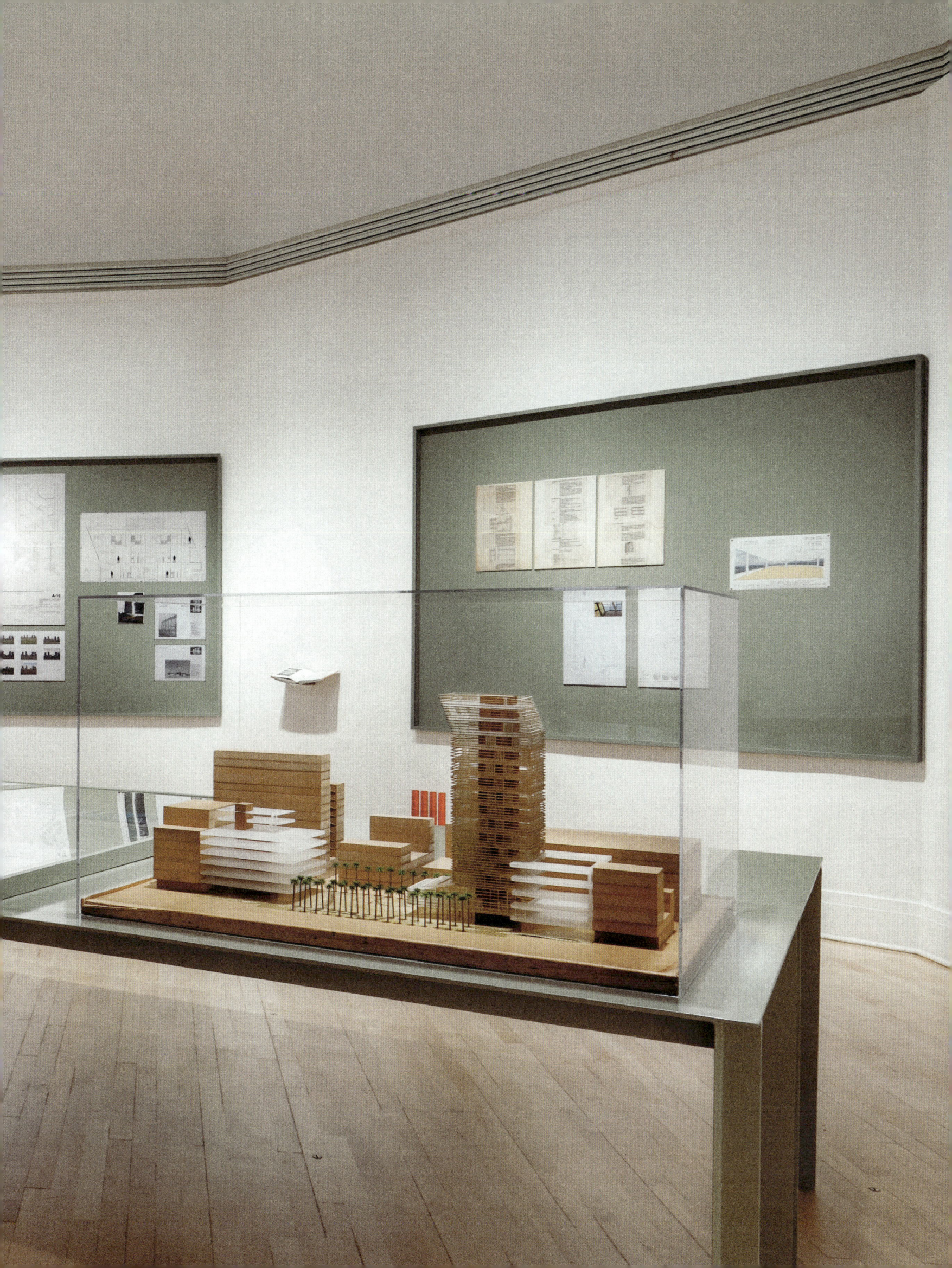

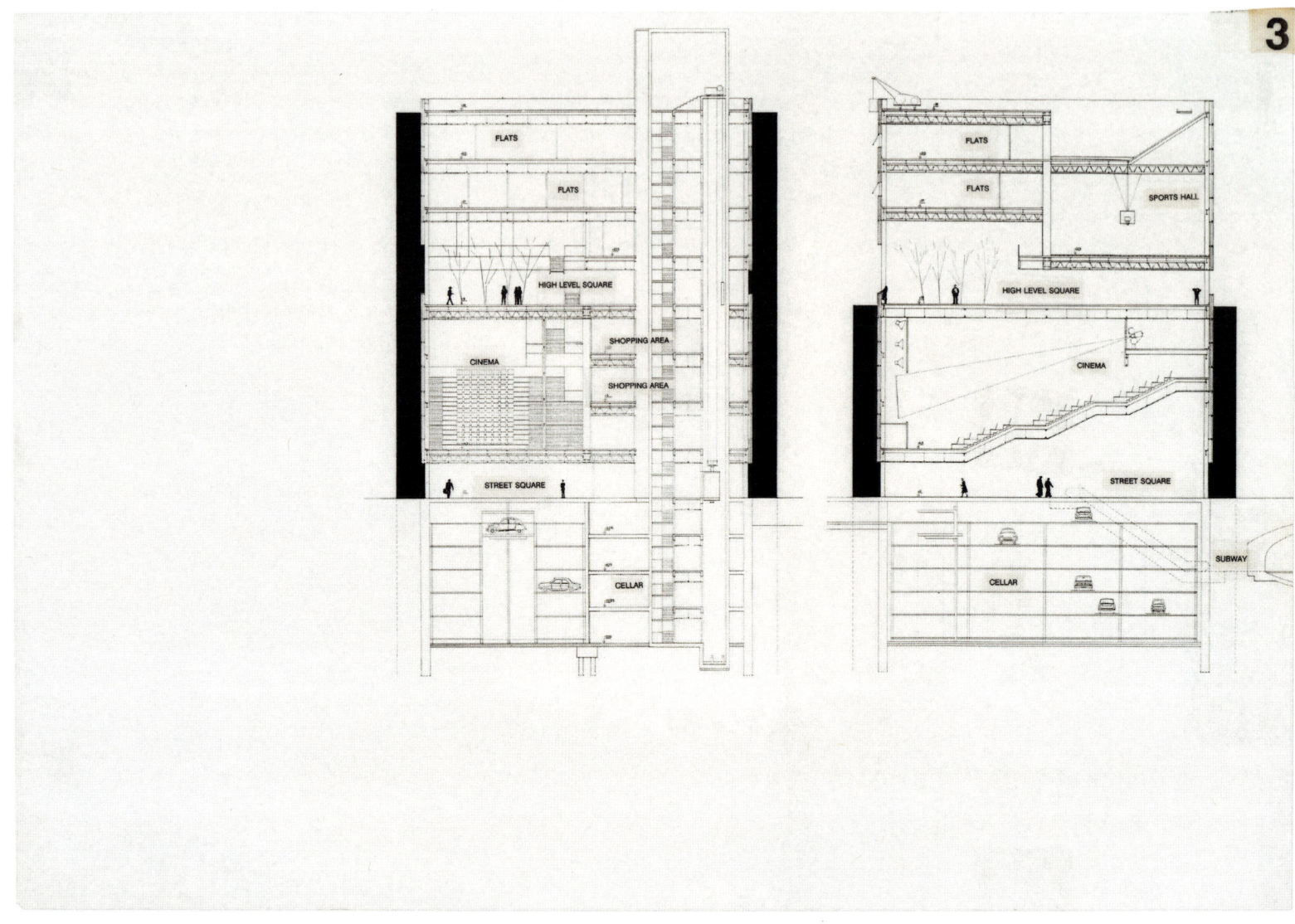

Above: Mock-up for a presentation panel for the Zephyr Competition self-sufficient hybrid towers showing sections of tower and program layout, 1994. Collage of electrostatic prints, printed number and tape on translucent paper, 42 × 59.4 cm.
AP164.S1.1994.D2.ARCH271747

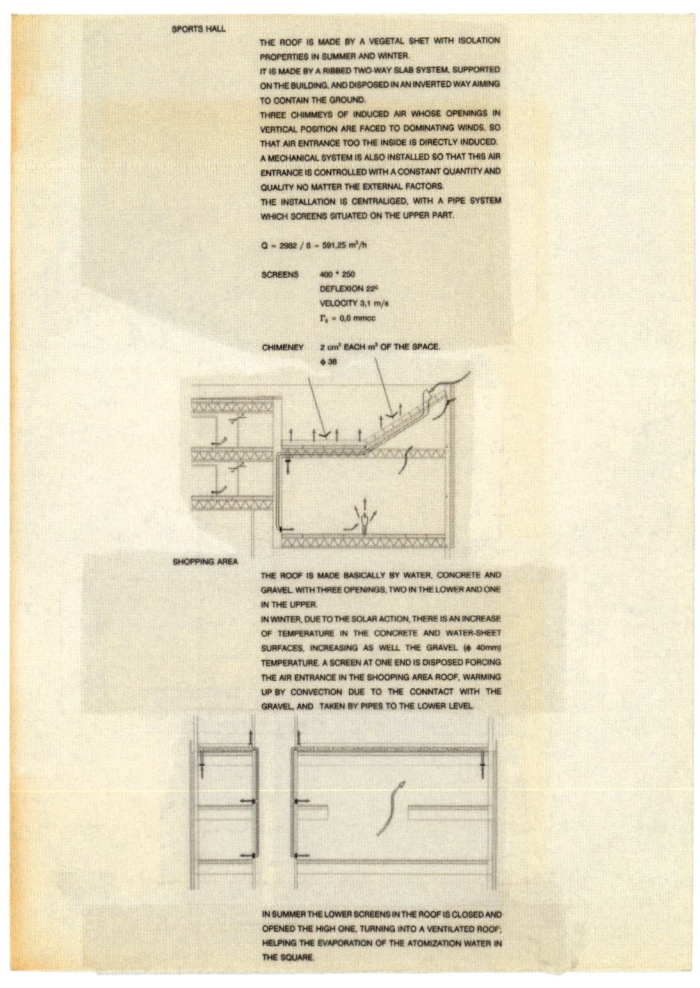

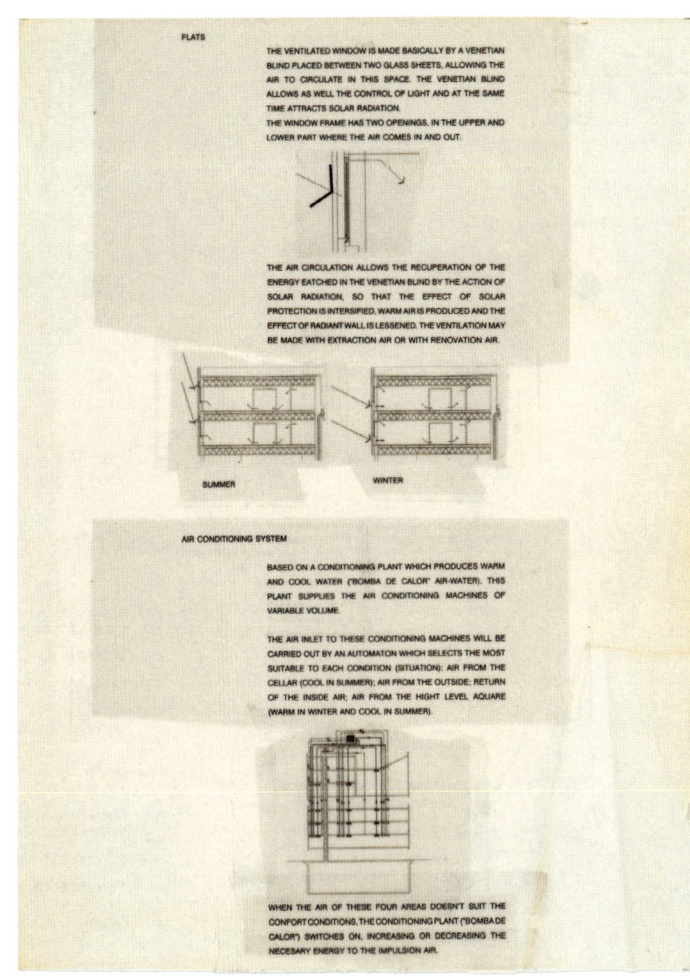

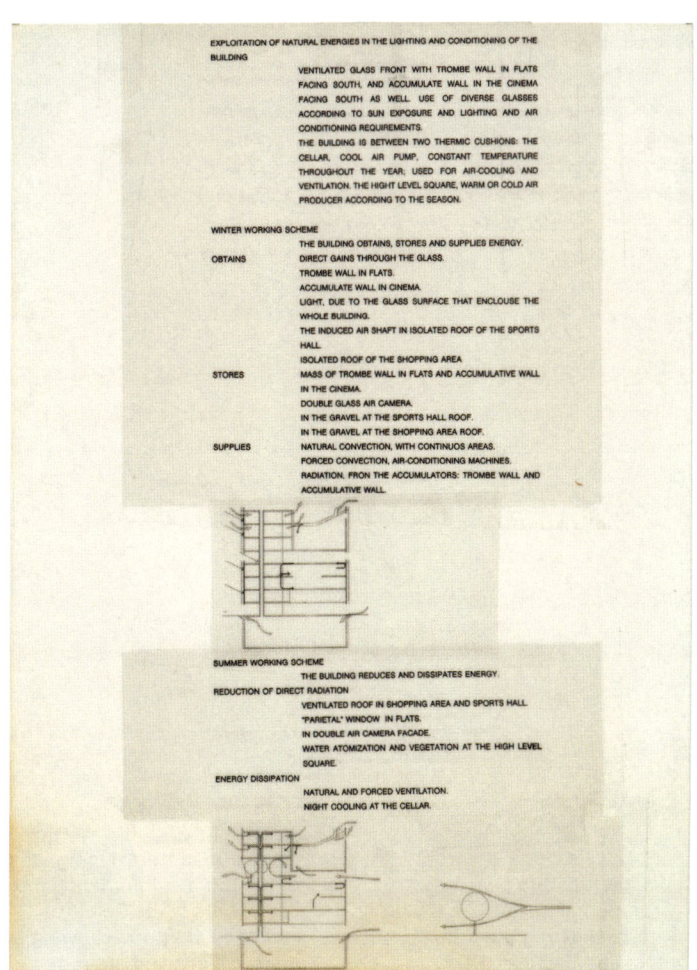

Above, left: Mock-up for a presentation panel for the Zephyr Competition self-sufficient hybrid towers describing the climatic properties of the roof structures of the sports hall and shopping area in winter and summer, 1994. Collage of electrostatic prints, black ink and tape on translucent paper, 29 × 29.7 cm. AP164.S1.1994.D2.ARCH271741

Above, right: Mock-up for a presentation panel for the Zephyr Competition self-sufficient hybrid towers describing the bioclimatic strategy of the tower facades in winter and summer, 1994. Collage of electrostatic prints and tape on translucent paper, 41.8 × 29.7 cm. AP164.S1.1994.D2.ARCH271743

Left: Mock-up for a presentation panel for the Zephyr Competition self-sufficient hybrid towers describing the ventilation system of the windows in the living units and the air-conditioning system throughout one of the towers, 1994. Collage of electrostatic prints and tape on translucent paper, 41.8 × 29.7 cm. AP164.S1.1994.D2.ARCH271744

Juan José Castellón González

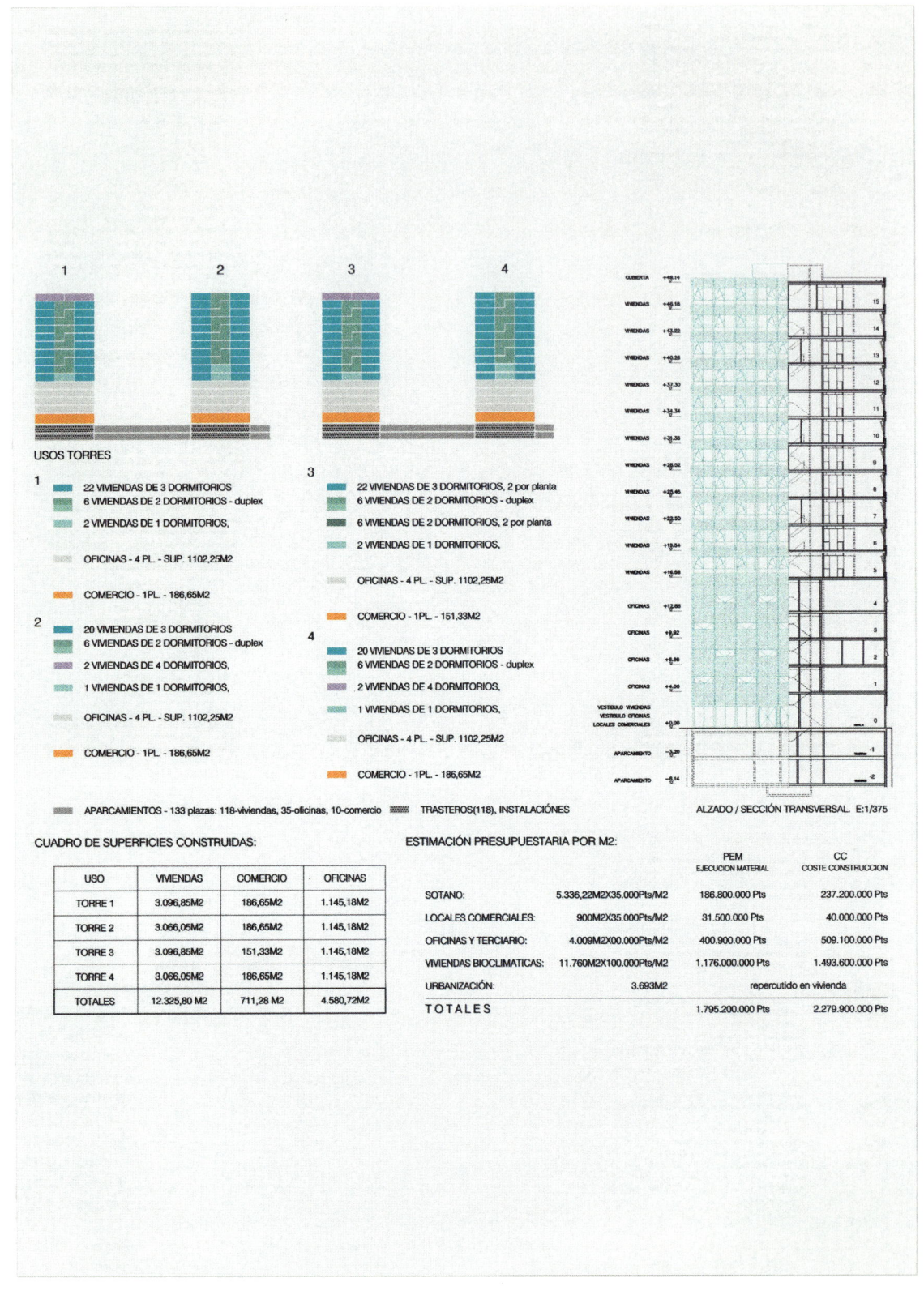

Above: Section of one of the environmental mixed-use towers in the Salburua wetlands in Vitoria, and diagrammatic studies calculating program layout and area, c. 2001–2006. Digital print, 31.8 × 22.4 cm.
AP164.S1.2002.D2.ARCH271716

Opposite, top: Site plan for the environmental mixed-use towers in Vitoria showing the urban context and Salburua Park, a wetland habitat, c. 2001–2006. Electrostatic print, 21 × 29.7 cm.
AP164.S1.2002.D2.ARCH271750:055

Opposite, bottom: Floor plans of the four environmental mixed-use towers in the Salburua wetlands in Vitoria showing living units, offices and ground-floor retail space, c. 2001–2006. Ink-jet print, 29.7 × 42 cm.
AP164.S1.2002.D2.ARCH272319

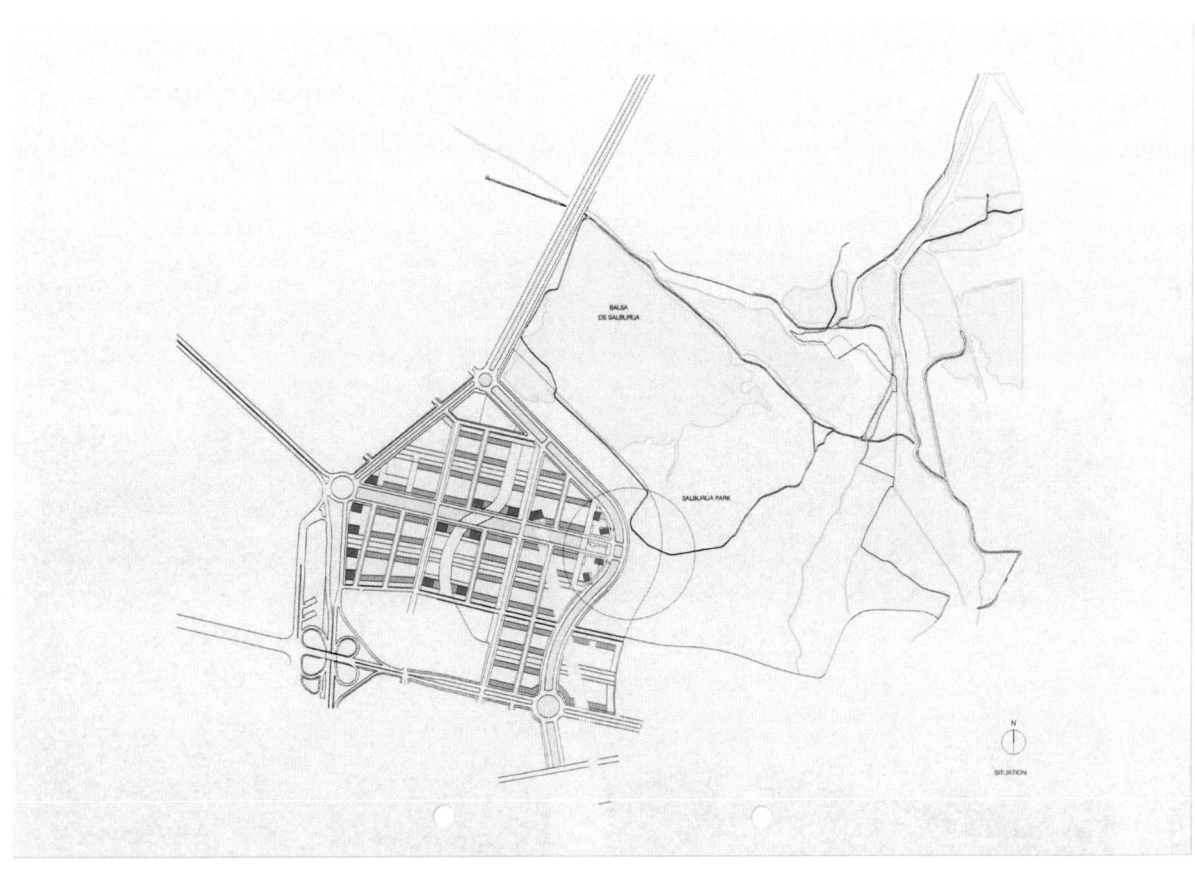

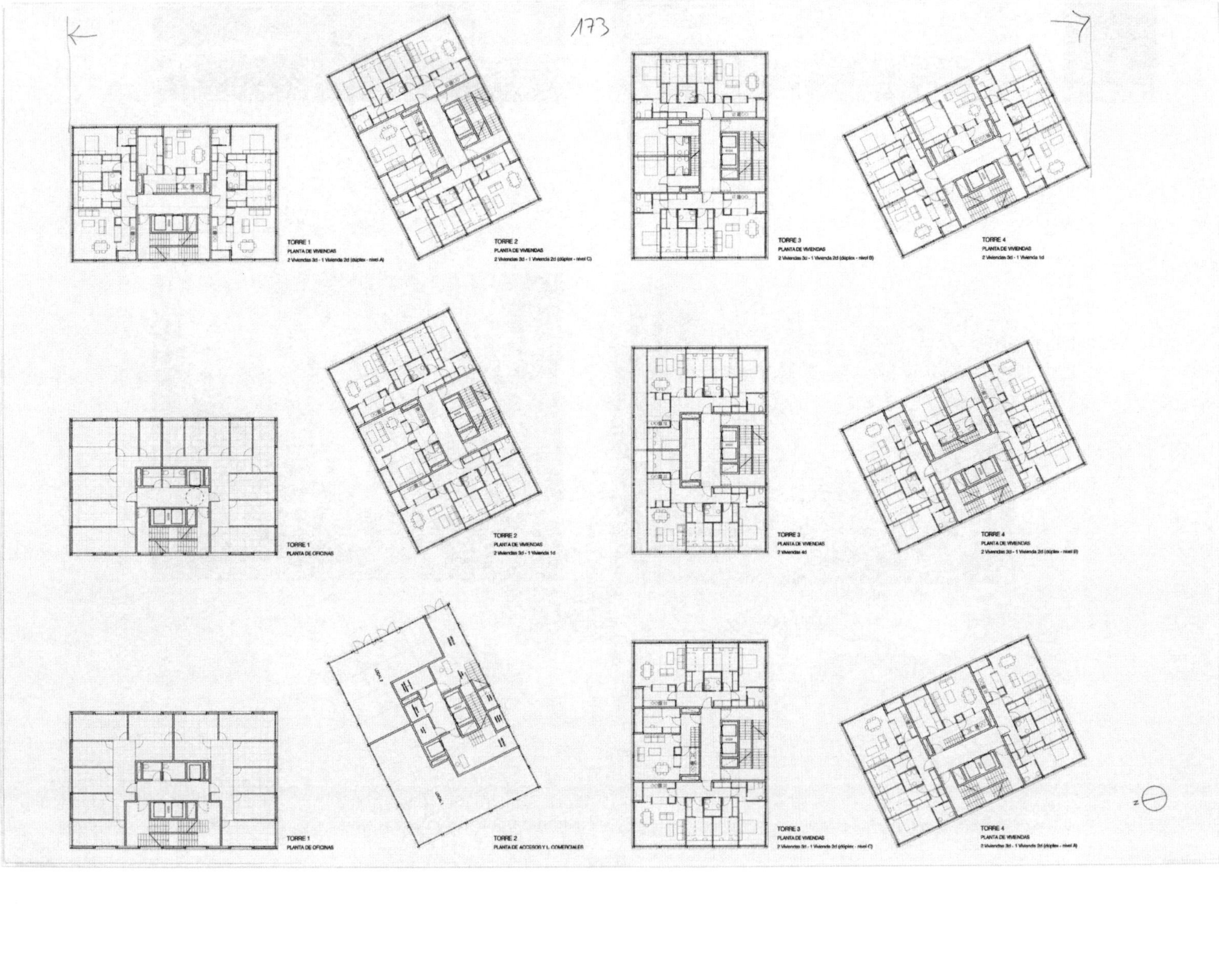

Above: Construction views of the environmental-mixed use towers showing the access road and surrounding wetlands in Vitoria, 2005. Ink-jet print, 29.7 × 42 cm. AP164.S1.2002.D2.ARCH271750:049

Opposite: Diagrams of tower shadows and energy-harnessing areas for the environmental mixed-use towers in the Salburua wetlands in Vitoria, c. 2001–2006. Digital print, 31.8 × 22.5 cm. AP164.S1.2002.D2.ARCH271719

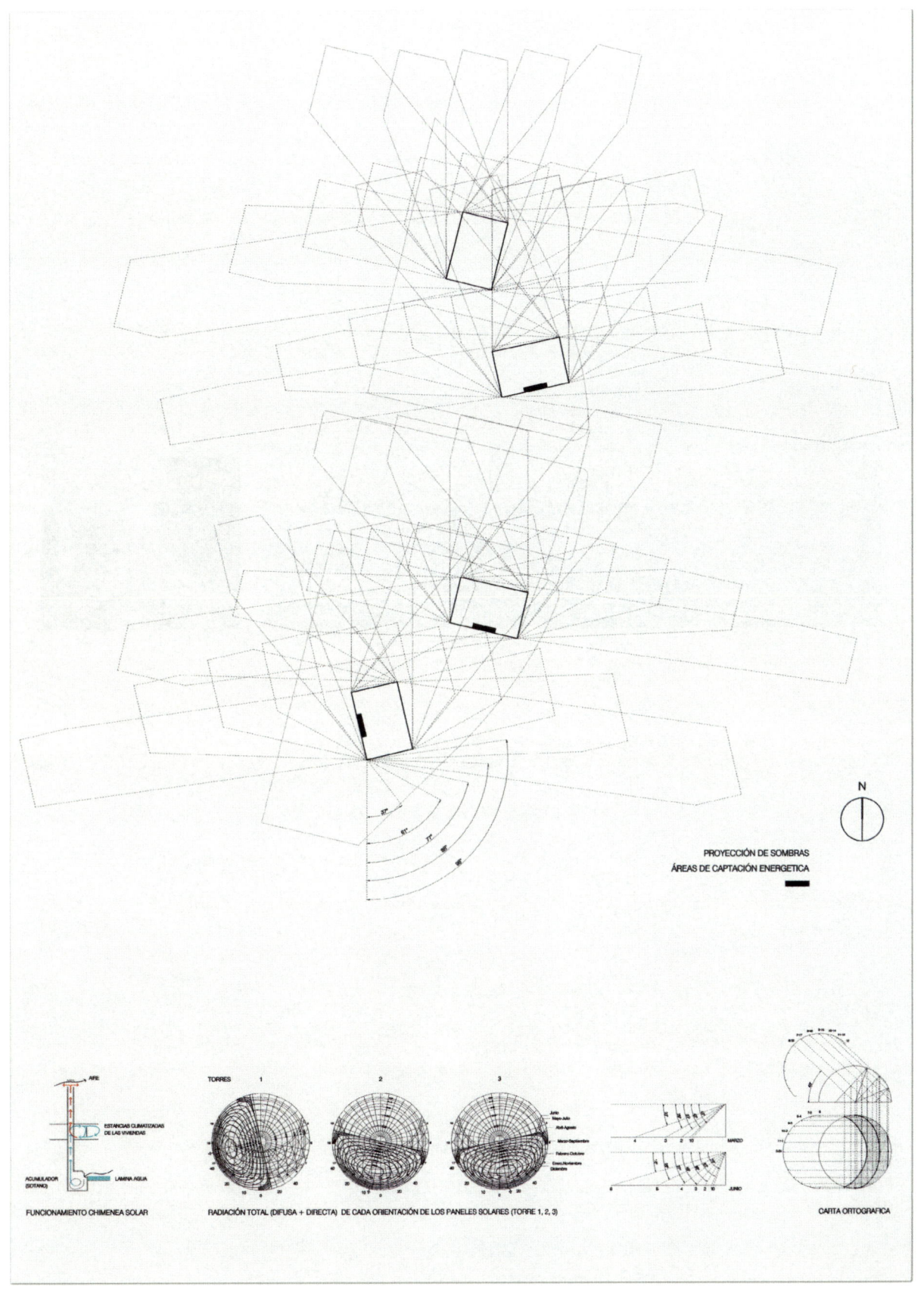

PROYECCIÓN DE SOMBRAS
ÁREAS DE CAPTACIÓN ENERGETICA

FUNCIONAMIENTO CHIMENEA SOLAR | RADIACIÓN TOTAL (DIFUSA + DIRECTA) DE CADA ORIENTACIÓN DE LOS PANELES SOLARES (TORRE 1, 2, 3) | CARTA ORTOGRAFICA

Juan José Castellón González

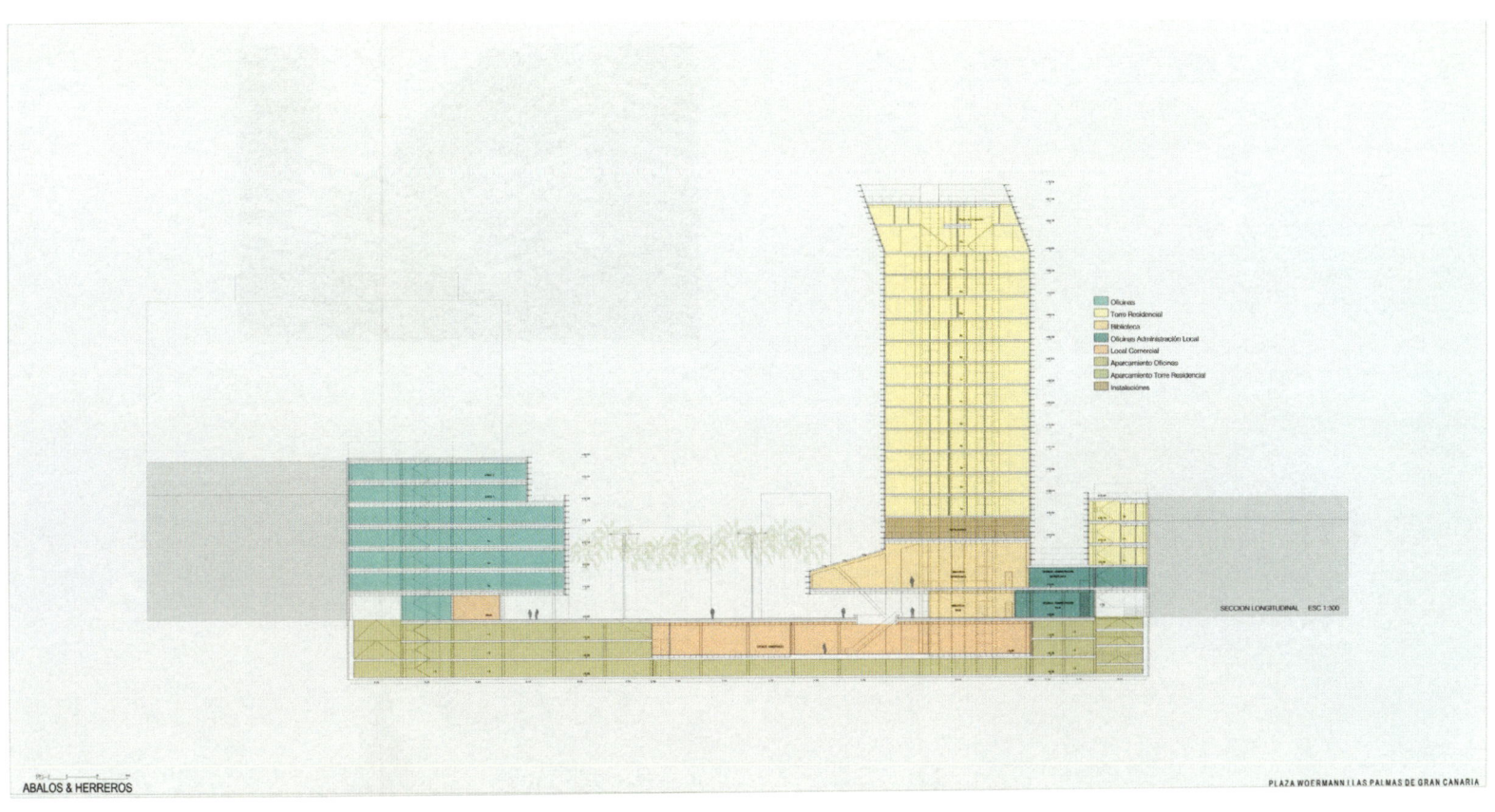

Opposite: Views showing the beachfront and isthmus of Las Palmas de Gran Canaria, and sketches of the design of the Woermann Plaza and Tower, c. 2005. Ink-jet print, 42 × 29.7 cm. AP164.S1.2001.D7.ARCH272021

Top: Longitudinal section of the Woermann Plaza and Tower showing program layout, c. 2001–2005. Ink-jet print, 42 × 80.2 cm. AP164. S1.2001.D7.ARCH272005

Above: Rooftop and floor-plan typologies of the Woermann Tower, c. 2001–2005. Ink-jet print, 46 × 61.9 cm. AP164.S1.2001.D7.ARCH271712

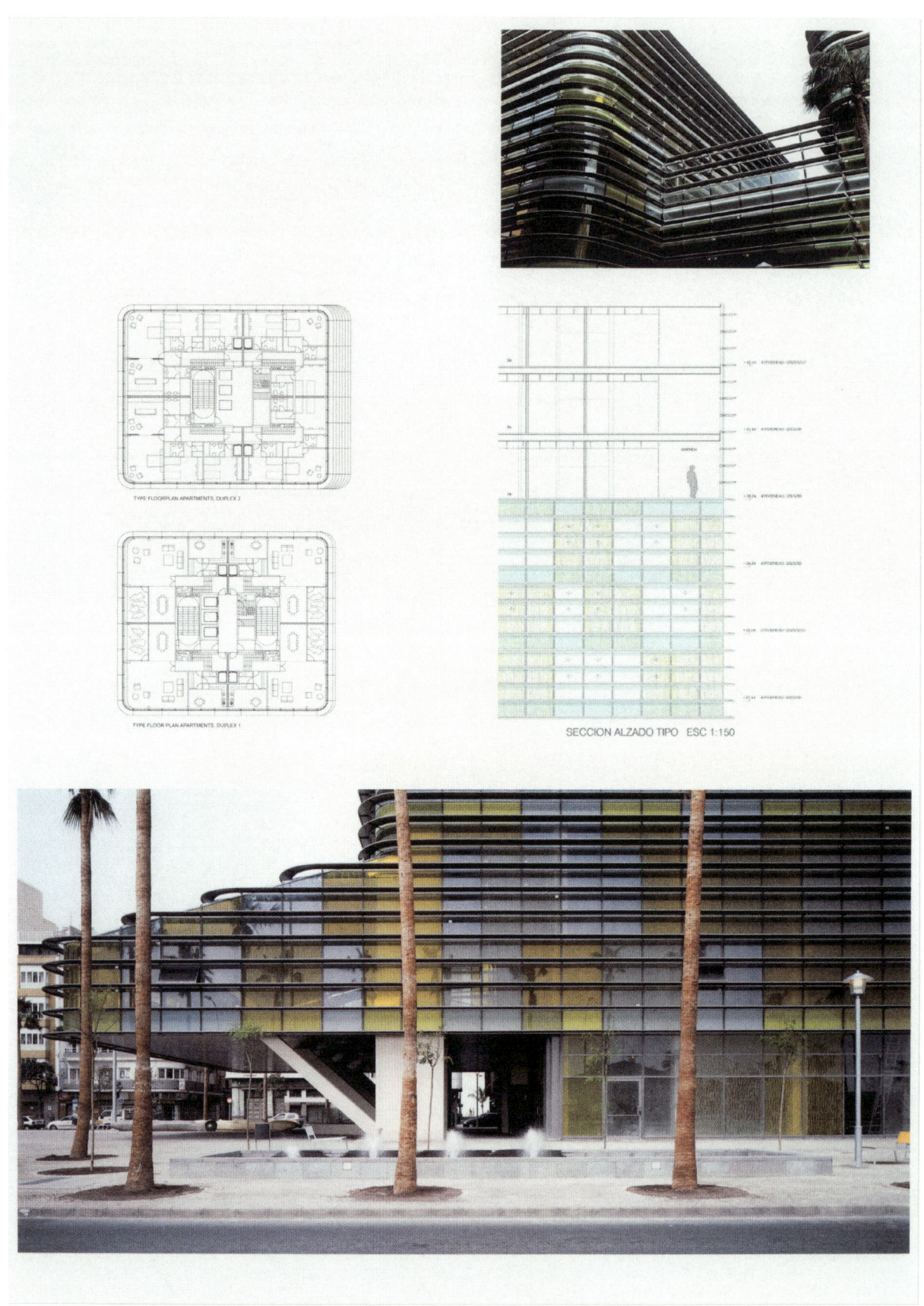

Above: Page layout showing floor plans, section and partial views of the Woermann Tower, c. 2005. Ink-jet print, 42 × 29.7 cm. AP164.S1.2001.D7.ARCH271723

Opposite: Photomontaged view of the Woermann Plaza and Tower nearing completion, c. 2004. Chromogenic colour prints, 18.6 × 15.7 cm. AP164.S1.2001.D7.ARCH271720

Juan José Castellón González

Studies for a plant motif for windows of the Woermann Tower, c. 2001–2005. Ink-jet print, 29.7 × 21 cm. AP164.S1.2001.

D7.ARCH272010, AP164.S1.2001.
D7.ARCH272013, AP164.S1.2001.
D7.ARCH272011, AP164.S1.2001.
D7.ARCH272014

May 2015

Juan José Castellón González unpacks his research methodology and curatorial strategy. Comments by Iñaki Ábalos and Juan Herreros appear in red.

• Juan Herreros: I remember students asking us about what to do after finishing their studies, or asking us for letters of reference to work with famous architects. We told them: "Don't go to work with a famous architect. Go to work with an architect who is only ten years older than you, who is halfway to being something that you could perhaps be one day. Don't go to work with a master, because systems of working will change so fast in the near future that perhaps what you learn there will not help you in your later career."

•• JH: *Jai tech* is a kind of fun tech, but *jai* is a word with different meanings, including a tongue-in-cheek Spanish pronunciation of "hi." *Jai tech* is a way of saying, "Hello, tech," or "Welcome," irreverently.

••• Iñaki Ábalos: This was a time of production. It was the only moment that was relatively successful. What this reading of the archive does not show is how much we worked, how many projects failed and how many projects we were not paid for. This was the first time we were building two or three projects at once. It was indeed a happy time.

Juan José Castellón González: Working with Ábalos&Herreros was my first job as an architect. I was there for four very intense years: from 2003 until 2007. My school in terms of the academy was at the universities in Barcelona and Madrid, but my school as an architect was with Ábalos&Herreros. This is also the case for a generation of architects who came of age in their office. Being part of an office with the chance to experience all levels of the architectural process gave me a unique opportunity to understand practice.

• I also had the chance to work onsite, where I faced real problems and experienced the complexity of architecture first hand. In the archive at the CCA, I found drawings that I made, and emails and faxes with my name on them. I may have even done some of the drawings selected for the exhibition; at Ábalos&Herreros there was no sense of individual authorship. But it would be impossible for me to discuss the office from a distance, because I was there and I still feel that I am somehow a small part of this history.

In the exhibition I want to express the transition from theory to practice, which is crucial in the work of Ábalos&Herreros. Particularly important is the light attitude that Ábalos&Herreros adopted to make this transition. Lightness can be analyzed from many different perspectives, but Ábalos&Herreros interpreted it as an attitude in the face of complexity. We live in an extremely complex environment, surrounded by computers and other new technologies. Similarly, architecture is in itself a complex practice that involves many elements and implies a great deal of responsibility. But Ábalos&Herreros showed that this complexity can be faced with lightness. In their book *Areas of Impunity*, they define the concept of *jai tech* as an alternative to high tech, which implies building higher and building more, resulting in buildings that are containers for productivity. Following the jai-tech philosophy, Ábalos&Herreros instead saw the tower as a laboratory for human interaction and a container for social activity. I think this approach is much more closely connected to technique than to technology. It relates to the use and the evolution of techniques, both traditional and contemporary, which go beyond the application of technology and complex systems.

•• But the office was small. From 2003 until 2007 there were between twelve and twenty people working on four or five projects simultaneously. It was an intense time and we had to face complexity with minimal resources. Without understanding its limits and being able to develop strategic thinking, it would have been impossible for an office of this size to work on such big projects. Lightness was only possible through the definition of strategies and the elaboration of an architecture that broke up the complexity into simpler pieces that were affordable, understandable, easy to communicate and easy to apply to different projects at different scales.

••• The exhibition focuses on three projects. Two projects are the towers that were built during the time that I worked in the office: the mixed-use towers in Vitoria and the Woermann Tower. The project for the self-sufficient hybrid towers, on the other hand, became a kind of manifesto that involved many of the ideas that were developed further in later projects.

The exhibition is organized according to five strategies. The first is the contextual strategy, which shows how the building reacts to the environment, as if it were a human body. For example, the mixed-use towers in Vitoria rotate and accommodate their position according to views, projected shadows, questions of access and other parameters. The use of glass and the fact that the towers are isolated and rotated create striking views of the surroundings, so the quality of the outside space is brought inside. The intention to bring nature into the building is also present in other projects: in the Woermann Tower, in Casa Verde and in the gymnastics pavilion in Retiro Park. In case of the Woermann Tower, the building makes a topological gesture, twisting and bending in dialogue with the environment. These operations can be regarded as part of a general strategy that was applied in different ways according to the context.

Juan José Castellón González

01

• JH: This work is connected to some texts that we wrote at a time when we were losing competitions and our projects were not being built. When we started building larger-scale projects, the theories and critical positions that we had written about before—many of them very ironic—became possible in built form.

•• JH: When we started doing larger-scale projects, especially the competitions that we won and the projects we were able to build, like the Ecoparc in Barcelona, the Woermann Tower and the Vitoria Towers—this is the moment at which our interest in gaining new information about industrial products through catalogues was transformed into a kind of culture.

I am not opposed to the word *complexity*, but it could be confusing. We are actually talking about a sophisticated simplicity. The operation that we did to eliminate a construction fetish in the production of these buildings is important.

I think that the work we did is relevant today because the production of architecture has

The site photographs show how important it was to understand the environment and the relationship between the natural and the artificial, which is present across the work of Ábalos&Herreros. These photomontages show a light attitude toward technique. Lightness defines the decision making and the control of the project, and it is also present in the technique itself. → Fig. 01

The second strategy is the programmatic strategy. It is connected to Ábalos&Herreros's concern with introducing social interaction into the program and articulating space in a balanced way. The picture of the model shows an articulation of the program and suggests a holistic approach to architecture that merges program with structure and space. And the section of the hybrid towers brings public interaction and social space into the building. It introduces the complexity of the city and condenses the different layers of information into an internal solution. → Figs. 02–03

It is important to see how this strong theoretical position is translated into practice, through an effort to bring the idea of the hybrid and the richness of spatial figuration from the public into the semi-public and private programs. And even though these documents correspond to different projects, they can be read as a whole. There is consistency in the way that these principles were translated into real construction.

•

The third strategy is the structural strategy. For Ábalos&Herreros, construction systems were especially important because of the catalogue's relevance for construction. Using the catalogue as a source of solutions or strategies to assemble the building was another way to confront complexity.

••

02–03

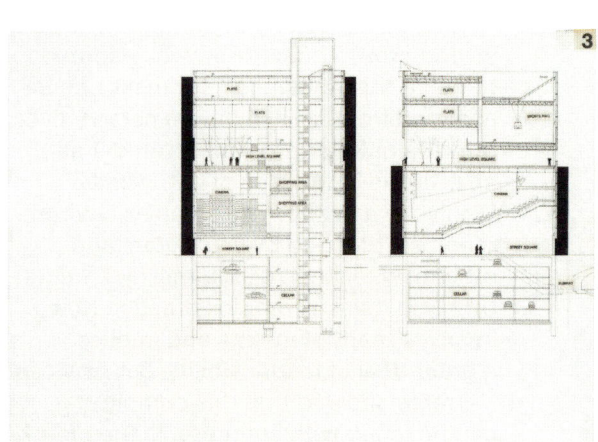

Fig. 01: Photomontage of a panoramic view from one of the environmental mixed-use towers in the Salburua wetlands in Vitoria, c. 2001–2006. Digital image. AP164.S1.2002.D2.ARCH276125 / Fig. 02: Photographic sequence of a study model showing the program and structure of the Zephyr Competition self-sufficient hybrid towers, 1994. Chromogenic colour prints, 8.1 × 21 cm. AP164.S1.1994.D2.ARCH271736, AP164.S1.1994.D2.ARCH271737, AP164.S1.1994.D2.ARCH271735 / Fig. 03: Mock-up for a presentation panel for the Zephyr Competition self-sufficient hybrid towers showing sections of a tower and program layout, 1994. Collage of electrostatic prints, a printed number and tape on translucent paper, 42 × 59.4 cm. AP164.S1.1994.D2.ARCH271747

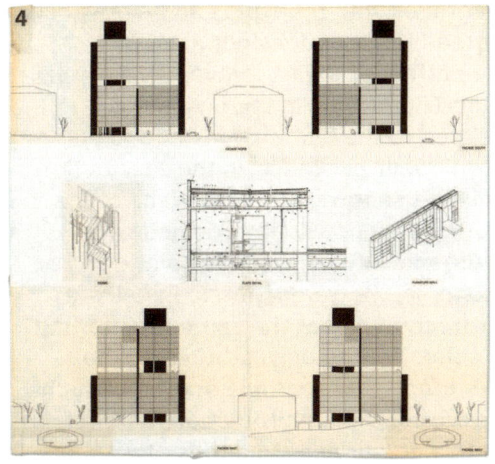
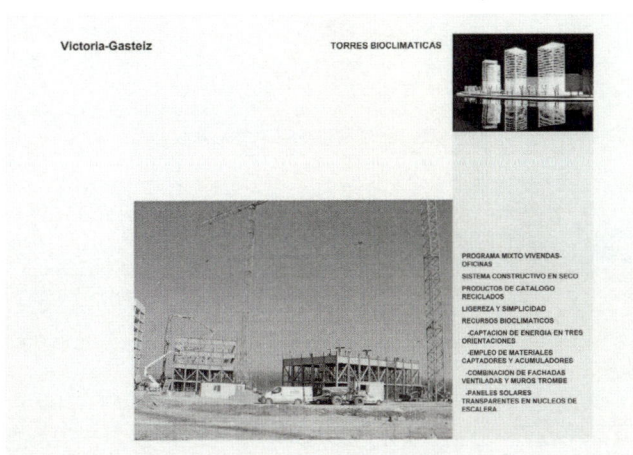

04–05

become such a complicated thing. It is still important to reduce equations and to look for simplicity in a project. That is perhaps the best aspect of the heritage of the twenty or so years we worked together: the ability to be pragmatic and to accept the many contingencies of architecture practice.

••• IA: The ingredients like the hybrid come from the use of catalogues as creative resources. We did not go to construction fairs so often, but for two or three years we went to Construmat in Barcelona and to Bâtimat in Paris. We looked through what was for sale and tried to pick things and put them together. It was so joyful. These fairs introduced us to the hybrid and the ready-made—things that were already there, that were juxtaposed and connected in new and surprising ways. This experience made boring things become exactly the opposite. It gave everything the potential to be enjoyed and allowed us to construct creatively instead of fighting against regulations.

JH: Today it is difficult for young architects—and for architects in general—to work in the mode of designing a building and building it, then designing another one and building it, and picking up the phone to accept another commission for a house. The archive of our much-admired Álvaro Siza at the CCA corresponds to the life of an architect in a small city who receives a call every three months from someone who wants a house. That way of working is going to disappear.

In contrast to this, unsuccessful competitions and invented commissions can help to advance new ways of being an architect. Many architects, especially young ones, build projects from time to time, and in between they publish, they write, they teach and they create things that go nowhere. But all of that is really what makes architecture move forward.

These conventional solutions were translated into the building and interpreted in a specific context. In the office we were working at a high level of detail, trying to understand all the elements to be assembled onsite and their connection across projects. For Ábalos & Herreros, recycling was not just a concept, but a real practice.

•••

A section of one of the hybrid towers shows how important it was to be precise: to describe all the elements involved in the definition of the technical section. It also shows the connection to other projects through the use of polycarbonate or glass. → Fig. 04

Ábalos & Herreros accumulated knowledge from project to project, which allowed the office to manage this volume of work at the same time.

Lightness was found onsite as well: in the structure of the mixed-use towers in Vitoria, for example. Structural elements were assembled in a warehouse, transported to the site and then put in place by a crane that was operated by one person. The process looks quite simple and light, which evokes the way we were working in the office. → Fig. 05

The knowledge was in the system and in the strategy, and then one person carried it out.

The fourth strategy is the thermodynamic strategy. Considering that these projects were developed almost twenty years ago, it is quite impressive to see the extent to which this strategy is present in practices today. Ábalos & Herreros were pioneers in seeing the thermodynamic as a source of new interpretations of architectural practice. Here there is a bit of friction between theory and practice. The theory was quite advanced, but the fact that we worked with conventional systems and catalogues was a limitation to translating this theory into a real building. In the end, the thermodynamic strategy was based on approaching problems of radiation and ventilation with customized solutions. Today this would be called parametric, but computers were not fully implemented at the time we were working on these projects.

Fig. 04: Mock-up for a presentation panel for the Zephyr Competition self-sufficient hybrid towers showing facade elevations, axonometric views of a structural frame and furniture wall and a section detail of a living unit, 1994. Collage of electrostatic prints, drafting appliqué, pen and ink, graphite, a printed number and tape on translucent paper and drafting film, 42 × 59.4 cm. AP164.S1.1994.D2.ARCH271745 / Fig. 05: Construction view of the environmental-mixed use towers in the Salburua wetlands in Vitoria, c. 2005. Laser print, 21 × 29.7 cm. AP164.S1.2002.D2.ARCH271887:010

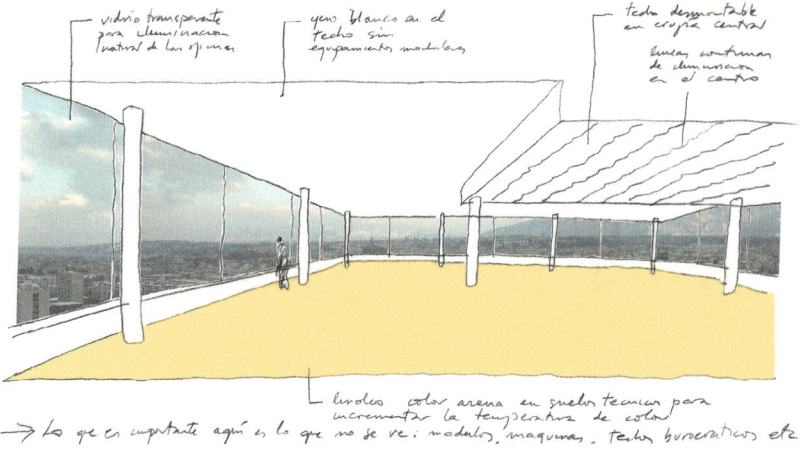

degrades with time and can be replaced, something that does not need to be perfect or to last forever. This understanding of time in the building is related to the human body and to our own fragile existence. In the case of the mixed-use towers in Vitoria, the office considered how to introduce design elements into very simple solutions. For example, we were trying to install fire protection and at the same time to find a colour for the polycarbonate panels. We found that a simple operation such as mixing the fire protection material with a colour achieved these two goals at once, giving texture and colour to a conventional system. It was creative but simple and inexpensive. → Fig. 07

• **JH: Our interest in catalogues was not a fascination with everything produced by the industry. What we were really looking for in these catalogues was a transposition of resources from one field into another. The accumulation of catalogues was perhaps necessary from a professional point of view because the Internet did not exist and we needed this material. But for us, catalogues were neutral publications in which the importance of the products seemed to depend on the user's intelligence and ability to discover new applications for them.**

We were looking for a kind of freedom: an understanding that all these products are available to be recombined to create a new lexicon.

The standard solution was based on machines. A perspective of the interior of one of the mixed-use towers in Vitoria has a note that says, "*Lo que es importante aquí es lo que no se ve*": "What is important here is what you cannot see," that is, modules, machines and ceilings. → Fig. 06

Inside the ceilings were machines that were meant to carry out solutions developed by architectural systems. This situation produced tension between the theory and the application of the real machines and the available technical systems. Now the catalogue is digital as well as physical, and everything can be customized. The strategy would be enacted differently today.

•

The last strategy is the superficial strategy. The term *superficial* is used intentionally because it introduces the idea of something that is not deep, but it is also connected with time and with fragility. Ábalos&Herreros defined the fragile skin as something that

In the case of the Woermann Tower, the intention was to experiment with glass on the facade. Different patterns were tested and were installed between two layers of glass. The goal was to avoid a literal connection between outside and inside, to establish a filter between the two and to combine the artificial and the natural in the architecture. → Fig. 08

In general, all five strategies could be merged, and in the exhibition the viewer can make connections between different aspects of each of the three projects. The theory is always present as a frame of reference for the material produced in the office.

Two more elements of the exhibition should be mentioned. First is the picture of Iñaki and Juan in their twenties. It is one of the first pictures that shows the two of them together, and it expresses their attitude toward architecture. They are looking out from the roof of the cathedral of Notre-Dame de Paris, enjoying the experience of being there. I think they still have this approach to their work. → Fig. 09

Second is a selection of songs that were often playing in the office; music helped to build the working environment of Ábalos&Herreros. In other offices, the music is often meant to increase productivity: they play techno or something like that. But at Ábalos&Herreros,

Fig. 06: Sketch of an interior view of one of the environmental mixed-use towers in the Salburua wetlands in Vitoria, c. 2001–2006. Digital drawing. AP164.S1.2002.D2.ARCH276126 / Fig. 07: View of one of the four environmental mixed-use towers in the Salburua wetlands in Vitoria, showing coloured spray-foam insulation, which was meant to be seen through translucent polycarbonate panels, c. 2001–2005. Digital image. AP164.S1.2002.D2.ARCH276127 / Fig. 08: Study for a plant motif for windows of the Woermann Tower, c. 2001–2005. Ink-jet print, 29.7 × 21 cm. AP164.S1.2001.D7.ARCH272016

09

When I revisited the definition, I decided that it explains my main point. Moreover, the choice to appropriate existing material connects to Ábalos & Herreros's use of the catalogue. The term *jai tech* is meant to formalize something that is already there. I was not looking through the books for content but was rather just trying to find the words and the concepts to express what I already knew from the practice. I think this is a credit to Ábalos & Herreros because the consistency between theory and practice in their work is remarkable. In a book that they wrote in the 1990s, I found the words to explain things that I experienced a decade later.

•• IA: I do not agree with the list of songs, actually. From the selection, I like the Super Furry Animals, Starsailor, the Jayhawks and maybe Fangoria. People were at risk of being rejected from the office if they brought bad CDs.

Music interested us because of the evidence of a design technique. Musicians are twenty or thirty years ahead of architects in terms of the use of technology for design. They make hybrids of analogue and digital music, and edit their work. We can learn a lot about the computer, the drawing and the collage through the way musicians work.

JH: There were two music players in the office: one was in the space that Iñaki and I worked in. We were interested in live music and we went to many concerts to look for approaches to immediate and efficient production that we could apply to our own work. Our interest in music was not a question of songs but rather of projects. We were more interested in the artists having a project, in terms of research into how to re-describe reality.

IA: I remember in the Quentin Tarantino film *Kill Bill* there is a short exchange about music:
"He's fond of music."
"Aren't we all?"
Everyone likes music. But for us, music was interesting because of the aesthetic of a pop song: two minutes and it lasts forever in your mind.

the music was mainly pop and it was almost always light. It generated an atmosphere of work and interaction that was an extension of our practice. The attitude of Ábalos & Herreros was non-dogmatic and I think working there gave you a certain freedom of expression that allows you to position yourself in architecture without having to judge everything you do.

••

One of the other things that I learned from Ábalos & Herreros is to not have a prejudiced view of words. The way Ábalos & Herreros used words was a rebellion against dogma in architecture. The term *superficial* in this context does not have a negative connotation. It is an acknowledgment of a reality: not all materials are expensive or last forever. In the Ecoparc in Barcelona, the panels are made of polycarbonate, which is not a complex material but is nevertheless an adequate solution. The panels need to be replaced over time, but the building still works.

Sense of humour was essential in the office and it is closely connected to the title of this exhibition. I can imagine that Iñaki and Juan had a lot of fun writing *Areas of Impunity*. I think most architects have a sense of humour, but not all of us are brave enough to show it. Not all architects would use terms like *jai tech*, *superficial* or *fragile*. To do this you need to be very confident in the work you are doing and in its position in your milieu.

In terms of the exhibition's title, jai tech is not something that I had in mind as I began the research in the archive, even though I had read *Areas of Impunity*.

Fig. 09: Invitation flyer for a lecture by Iñaki Ábalos and Juan Herreros at the Colegio Oficial de Arquitectos de Canarias, c. 1990. Electrostatic print, 11 × 16 cm. AP164.S2.SS2.ARCH270446

October 2014

Florian Idenburg and Jing Liu discuss objects they encounter during their research residency in the Ábalos&Herreros archive.

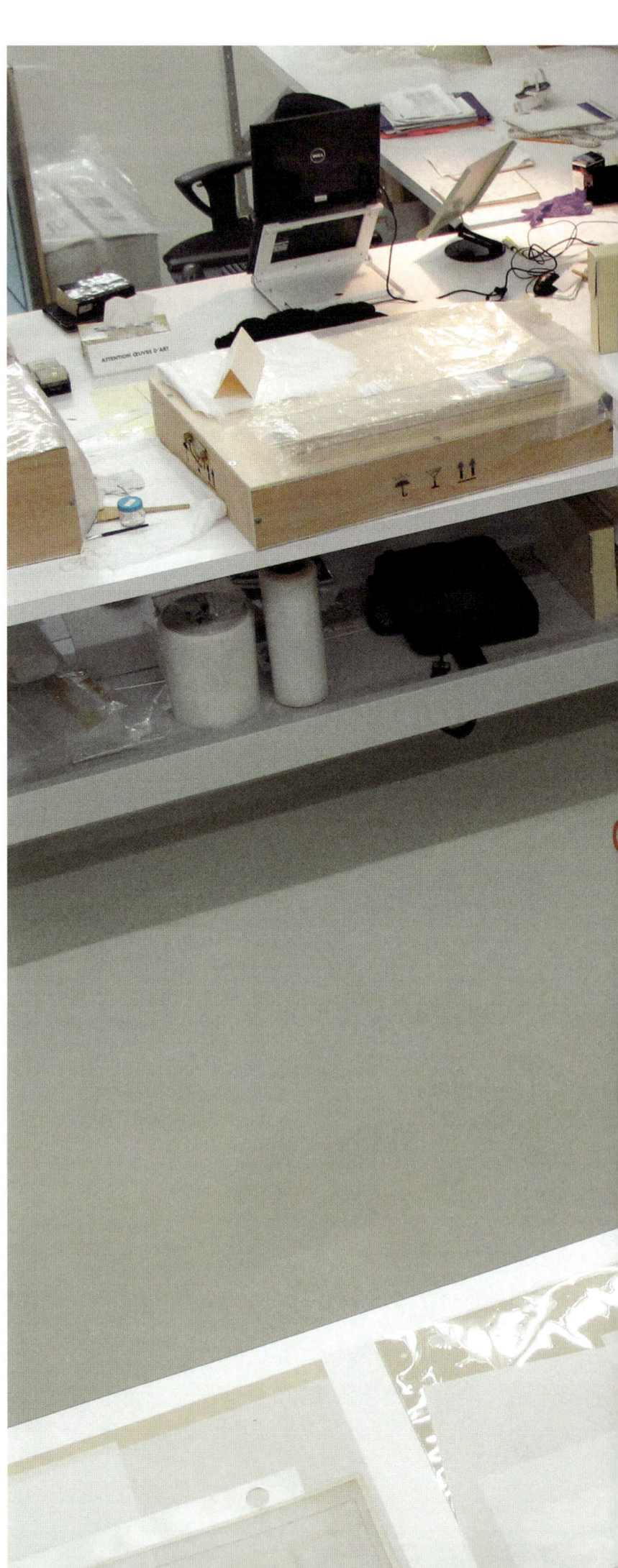

Florian Idenburg: Ábalos&Herreros identified new sites for architectural projects, as the Spanish landscape was transforming. An example is the project for a recycling plant in Valdemingómez, on the periphery of Madrid.

Jing Liu: Post-Franco Spain left something of a vacuum. Ábalos&Herreros found new territories where architecture had not previously been part of the conversation, neither culturally nor physically. They went to the outskirts of cities, to the beach and to recycling centres, and brought these landscapes into the architectural discussion. The landscapes resemble a tabula rasa, and in the face of such vast emptiness Ábalos&Herreros had to invent a role for architecture.

In the archive we found many photographs of site visits that show two men standing in these empty landscapes. There is something heroic about these images; they vividly illustrate the difference in scale between the landscape and the architects.

Top: Site panorama for the recycling plant for urban waste, Valdemingómez, c. 1996–1999. Ink-jet print on photographic paper, 21 × 29.7 cm.
AP164.S1.1996.D4.ARCH273197

Above: Photocopy of a site photograph for the recycling plant for urban waste, Valdemingómez, 1999. Electrophotographic print, 29.7 × 42 cm.
AP164.S1.1996.D4.ARCH276970

Florian Idenburg and Jing Liu

FI: Ábalos&Herreros took many pictures of these sites and then created collages to propose ways of inhabiting the land. This was at the very beginning of the era of Photoshop, when things were still done manually. In these collages, it is clear that they cut and pasted pictures from magazines as they imagined different ways of occupying the landscape, such as with race cars and pyramids.

There is a strong connection between the technique of representation and the technique of design. Both rely on appropriating existing elements and assembling a new landscape.

JL: When Ábalos&Herreros cut an element out of a car advertisement and inserted it into a new landscape like this, they gave a new meaning to a set of activities and rescribed contemporary life. They were quite inventive in proposing architectural interventions that could happen in this kind of landscape.

Top: Collage for the recycling plant for urban waste, Valdemingómez, c. 1996. Electrostatic prints, photo-offset lithographs and patterned drafting appliqué with marker, pressure-sensitive tape and corrections made in white correction fluid, 19.2 × 40.2 cm.
AP164.S1.1996.D4.ARCH271640

Bottom: Collage for the recycling plant for urban waste, Valdemingómez, c. 1996–1999. Electrostatic prints and coloured and patterned drafting appliqué, 28.9 × 40.8 cm.
AP164.S1.1996.D4.ARCH272898

FI: Many of these documents are photocopies. The photocopier was one of the main tools that Ábalos&Herreros used at the time, along with the scissors. Fundamentally, the technique of collage shows how they gave a new definition to peripheral landscapes. Where the land was once barren, now there are children in strollers and birds flying.

Photocopy of a collage for the recycling plant for urban waste, Valdemingómez, c. 1996. Graphite on a colour electrophotographic print, 29.7 × 42 cm.
AP164.S1.1996.D4.ARCH275387

Florian Idenburg and Jing Liu develop their research in the exhibition *Landscapes of the Hyperreal.*

Ábalos&Herreros
selected by

Florian Idenburg
and Jing Liu

23 July–13 September
2015

Landscapes of the
Hyperreal

Landscapes of the Hyperreal
Material included in the exhibition

View of the Ábalos&Herreros office,
Madrid, c. 2002
AP164.S3.D2.ARCH270449

Architectural characters

Sketches by Florian Idenburg and Jing Liu illustrating
architectural characters used by Ábalos&Herreros

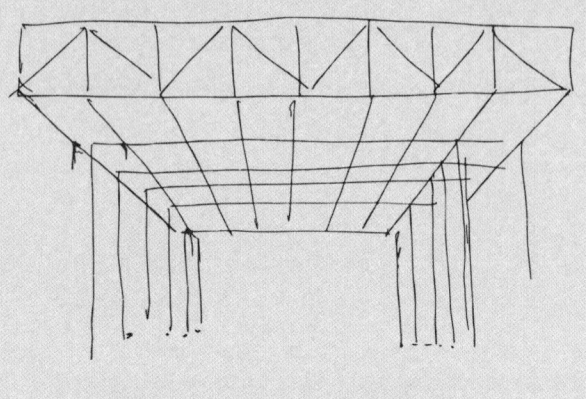

1. SHED

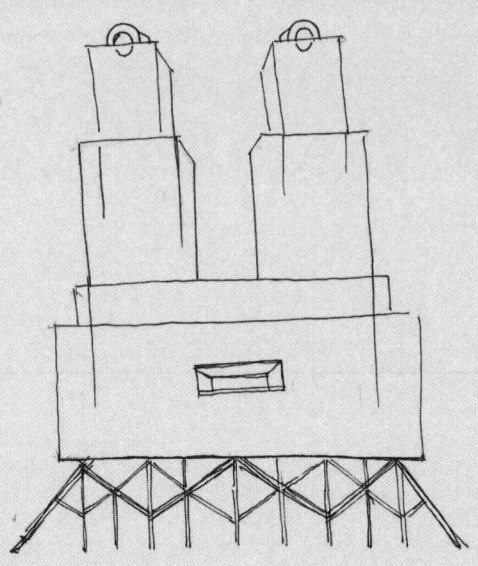

2. DOUBLE TOWER

3. ENVIRONMENTAL STRUCTURE

4. PATTERN

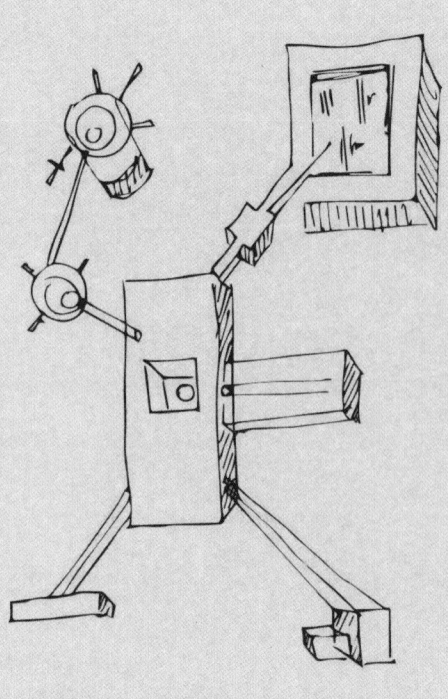

5. MACHINIC DEVICE

Architectural characters
Shed
Slide projection

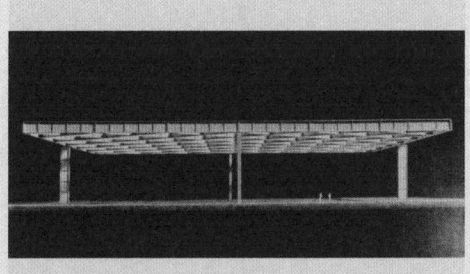

Meiji Watanabe
Steel Exhibition for the 1964 World's Fair. Master's thesis, Illinois Institute of Technology, 1960
AP164.S3.D2.ARCH273084

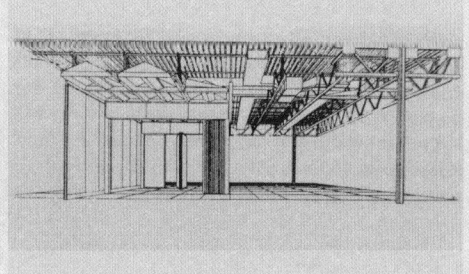

Ezra Ehrenkrantz
American School Construction Systems Development, 1962–1966
AP164.S3.D2.ARCH273063

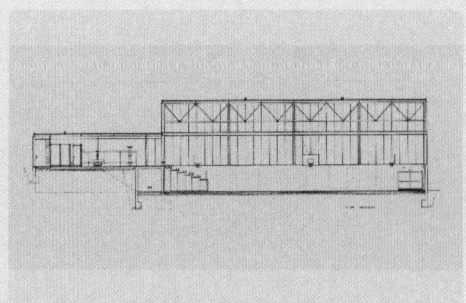

Ábalos&Herreros
#063. *Polideportivo Parquesol*
Parquesol sports hall, Valladolid, 1990
AP164.S1.1990.D2.ARCH270917

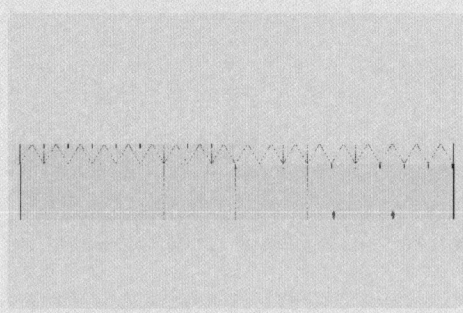

Ábalos&Herreros
#039. *Polideportivo y piscina cubierta*
Sports hall and indoor swimming pool, Vallecas, Madrid, 1986–1988
AP164.S1.1986.D1.ARCH276133

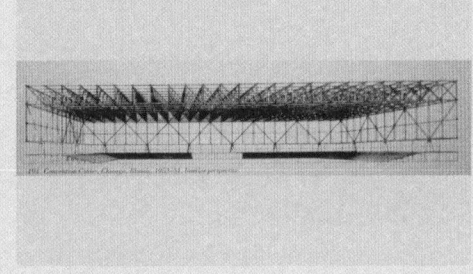

Mies van der Rohe
Convention Hall, Chicago, 1953
AP164.S3.D2.ARCH273086

Ábalos&Herreros
#094. *Biblioteca de Usera*
Usera library, Madrid, 1995–2003
AP164.S1.1995.D1.ARCH273068

Lawrence Kerry
Railway station for Chicago. Master's thesis supervised by Myron Goldsmith, Illinois Institute of Technology, 1968
AP164.S3.D2.ARCH273083

Ábalos&Herreros
#099. *Planta de reciclaje de residuos urbanos de Valdemingómez*
Recycling plant for urban waste, Valdemingómez, Madrid, 1996–1999
AP164.S1.1996.D4.ARCH273286

Herzog & de Meuron
Ricola Storage Building, Laufen, 1986
AP164.S3.D2.ARCH273054

Ábalos&Herreros
#067. *Polideportivo Madrigal de las Altas Torres*
Sports hall, Madrigal de las Altas Torres, Ávila, 1990
AP164.S1.1990.D6.ARCH277018

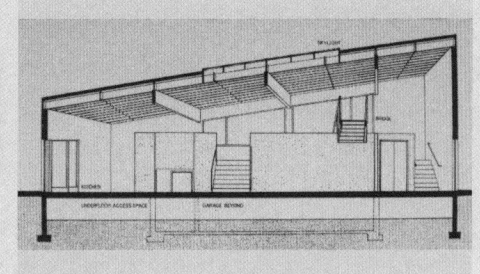

Frank Gehry
Davis Studio and Residence, Malibu, 1968–1972
AP164.S3.D2.ARCH273098

Ábalos&Herreros
#089. *Prototipos de vivienda industrializada: Casas AH-Gia*
Industrialized housing prototypes: AH-Gia Houses, 1993–1996
AP164.S1.1993.D11.ARCH273427

Architectural characters
Double Tower

Slide projection

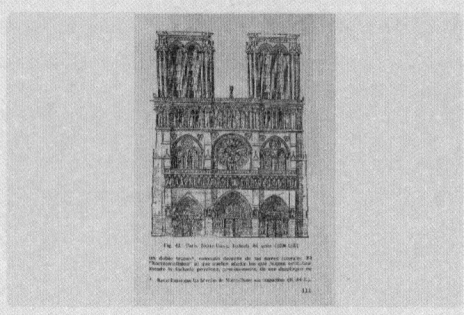

View of an elevation of the cathedral of Notre-Dame de Paris, 1163–1345

AHSO132R

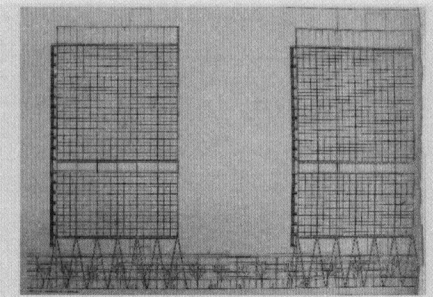

Ábalos&Herreros
#059. *Vivienda y ciudad, avenida Diagonal*
Housing and the City competition, Avinguda Diagonal, Barcelona, 1989

AP164.S1.1989.D4.ARCH270916

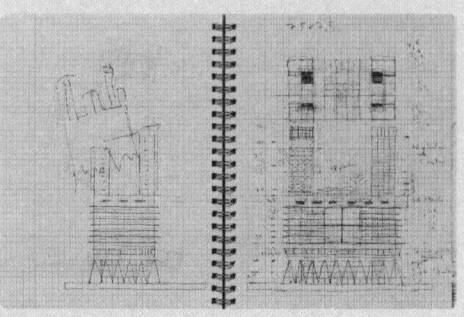

Ábalos&Herreros
#075. *Puerto Málaga*
Port of Málaga, 1992

AP164.S1.1992.D1.ARCH272892

Ábalos&Herreros
#082. *Encauzamiento del río Guadalhorce*
Channelling of the Guadalhorce River, Málaga, 1993

AP164.S1.1993.D4.ARCH277003

Ábalos&Herreros
#084. *Parque Dunar, Doñana*
Dune Park, Doñana National Park, 1993–1994

AP164.S1.1993.D6.ARCH272907

Ábalos&Herreros
#123. *El Mirador: torre mixta en la Bahía de Algeciras*
El Mirador: mixed-used tower on the Bay of Gibraltar, Algeciras, 1999

AP164.S1.1999.D10.ARCH277021

Emery Roth
The Eldorado, New York, 1931

AHSO135R

Bertrand Goldberg
Marina City, Chicago, 1959–1964

AP164.S3.D2.ARCH273094

Ábalos&Herreros
#123. *El Mirador: torre mixta en la Bahía de Algeciras*
El Mirador: mixed-used tower on the Bay of Gibraltar, Algeciras, 1999

AP164.S1.1999.D10.ARCH277021

Ludwig Hilberseimer
Chicago Tribune Building, 1922

AHSO133R

Architectural characters
Environmental Structure
Slide projection

Robert Le Ricolais
View of the Studio for Structural Investigation at the University of Pennsylvania, c. 1952
AP164.S2.SS3.D1.ARCH273055

Robert Le Ricolais
View of prototypes of spatial structures, c. 1952
AP164.S2.SS3.D1.ARCH273058

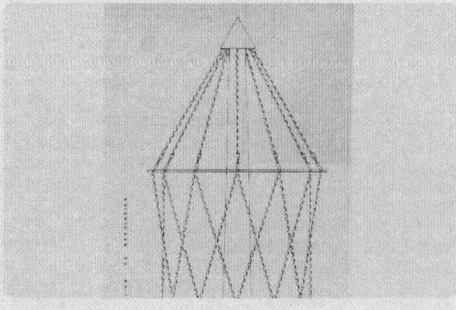

Ábalos&Herreros
#048. *Prototipo de estructura vertical*
Prototype for a vertical structure, Cáceres, 1987–1988
AP164.S1.1987.D3.ARCH273425

Toyo Ito
Tower of the Winds, Yokohama, 1986
AP164.S2.SS3.D1.ARCH273062

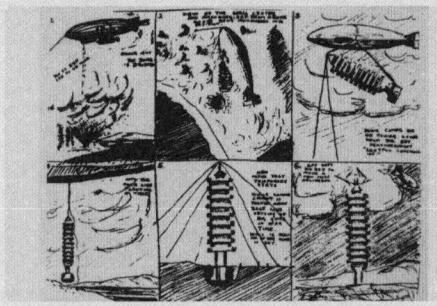

R. Buckminster Fuller
Light Tower, 1928
AP164.S3.D2.ARCH273073

Future Systems
Project 112: Coexistence Tower, 1984
AP164.S3.D2.ARCH273090

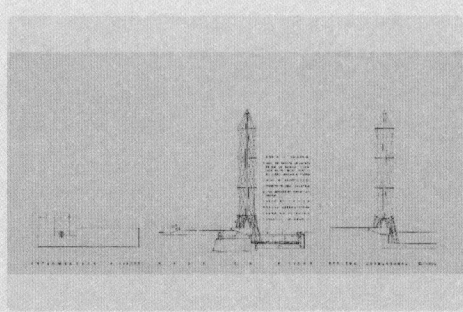

Ábalos&Herreros
#048. *Prototipo de estructura vertical*
Prototype for a vertical structure, Cáceres, 1987–1988
AP164.S1.1987.D3.ARCH273431

Ábalos&Herreros
#165. *Sagüés*
Sagüés: the gates of Ulía Park, San Sebastián, 2003
AP164.S1.2003.D5.ARCH276135

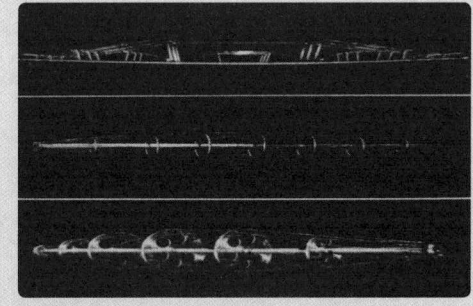

Robert Le Ricolais
View of prototypes of spatial structures, c. 1952
AP164.S2.SS3.D1.ARCH273056

Ábalos&Herreros
#099. *Planta de reciclaje de residuos urbanos de Valdemingómez*
Recycling plant for urban waste, Valdemingómez, Madrid, 1996–1999
AP164.S1.1996.D4.ARCH276134

Cedric Price
View of London Zoo Aviary, Regent's Park, c. 1965
DR2007:0077

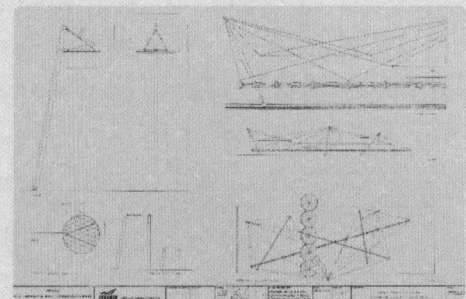

Ábalos&Herreros
#046. *Ordenación del nudo Puerta de Hierro*
Planning proposal for the Puerta de Hierro intersection, Madrid, 1987
AP164.S1.1987.D2.ARCH273282

Architectural characters
Pattern

Slide projection

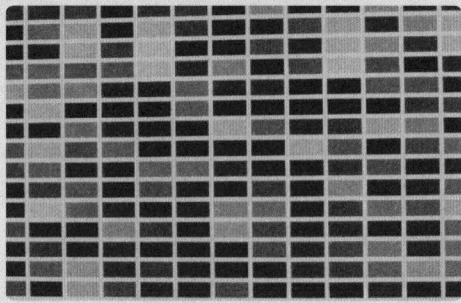

Gerhard Richter
Colour sample for a carpet commission, 1995
AP164.S3.D2.ARCH273069

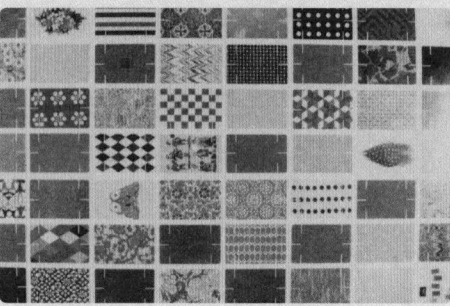

Charles and Ray Eames
Patterns, c. 1955
AP164.S3.D2.ARCH273078

Gerhard Richter
View of *1025 Farben* carpet, from the *Farben* series, c. 1970
AP164.S1.1995.D2.ARCH273283

Ábalos&Herreros
#106. *Recualificación del espacio público de Ramos*
Planning proposal for public space in Ramos, Rio de Janeiro, 1997–2003
AP164.S1.1997.D7.ARCH276136

Ábalos&Herreros
#106. *Recualificación del espacio público de Ramos*
Planning proposal for public space in Ramos, Rio de Janeiro, 1997–2003
AP164.S1.1997.D7.ARCH276137

Ábalos&Herreros
#106. *Recualificación del espacio público de Ramos*
Planning proposal for public space in Ramos, Rio de Janeiro, 1997–2003
AP164.S1.1997.D7.ARCH276139

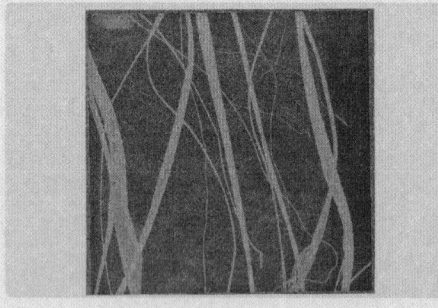

Ábalos&Herreros
#142. *Plaza y torre Woermann*
Woermann Plaza and Tower, Las Palmas de Gran Canaria, 2001–2005
AP164.S1.2001.D7.ARCH272013

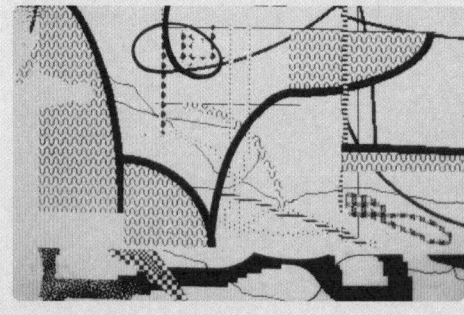

Albert Oehlen
View of a CAD painting, c. 1996
AP164.S3.D2.ARCH273076

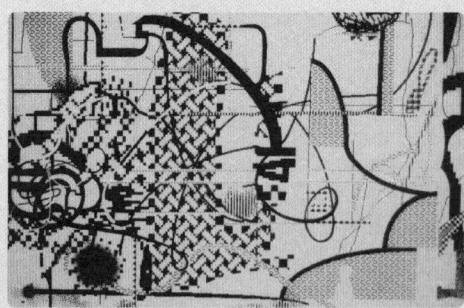

Albert Oehlen
View of a CAD painting, c. 1996
AP164.S3.D2.ARCH273075

Roberto Burle-Marx
Copacabana Beach promenade, Rio de Janeiro, 1970
AP164.S3.D2.ARCH273077

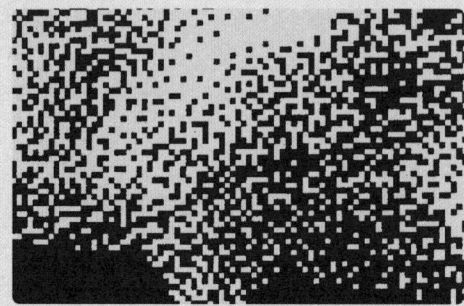

Ábalos&Herreros
#106. *Recualificación del espacio público de Ramos*
Planning proposal for public space in Ramos, Rio de Janeiro, 1997–2003
AP164.S1.1997.D7.ARCH276138

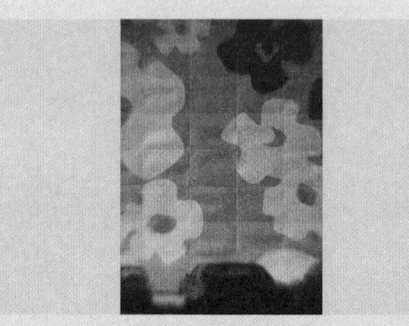

Robert Venturi and Denise Scott Brown
BEST Products Showroom, Langhorne, Pennsylvania, 1973–1979
AP164.S3.D2.ARCH273081

Architectural characters
Machinic Device
Slide projection

View of a nomadic structure carried by a donkey, n.d.
AP164.S3.D2.ARCH273096

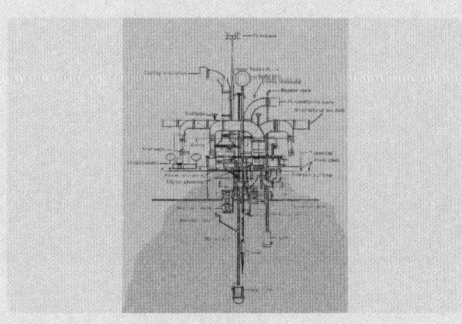

François Dallegret
Anatomy of a dwelling, illustration for Reyner Banham's "A Home Is Not a House," 1965
AP164.S3.D2.ARCH277004

Ron Herron/Archigram
Instant City, 1970
AP164.S3.D2.ARCH273080

Norman Foster and Partners
Furniture prototype, n.d.
AP164.S3.D2.ARCH273095

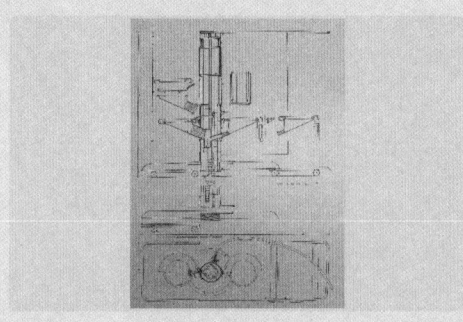

Ábalos&Herreros
#059. *Vivienda y ciudad, avenida Diagonal*
Housing and the City competition, Avinguda Diagonal, Barcelona, 1989
AP164.S1.1989.D4.ARCH277019

Richard Rogers
Furniture element, n.d.
AP164.S3.D2.ARCH273066

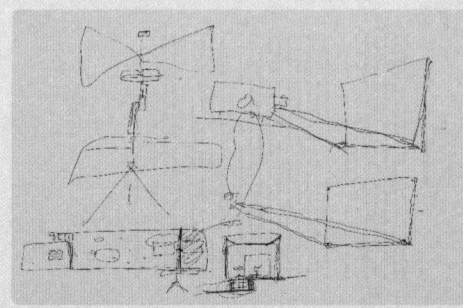

Ábalos&Herreros
#095. *III Bienal Arquitectura Española*
Third Biennial of Spanish Architecture and Urbanism, Comillas and Madrid, 1996–1997
AP164.S1.1995.D2.ARCH273284

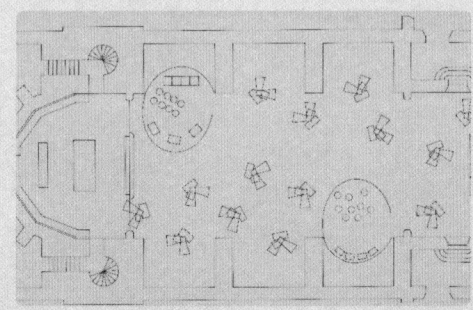

Ábalos&Herreros
#095. *III Bienal Arquitectura Española*
Third Biennial of Spanish Architecture and Urbanism, Comillas and Madrid, 1996–1997
AP164.S1.1995.D2.ARCH273104

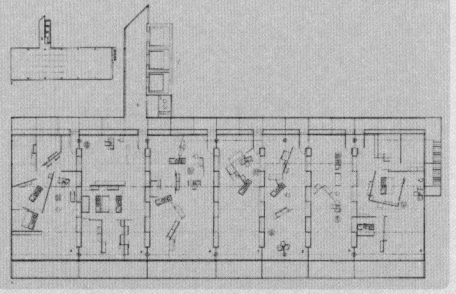

Ábalos&Herreros
#059. *Vivienda y ciudad, avenida Diagonal*
Housing and the City competition, Avinguda Diagonal, Barcelona, 1989
AP164.S1.1989.D4.ARCH277020

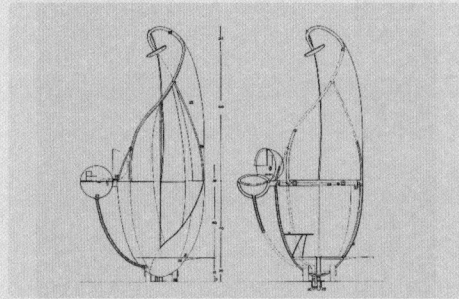

Ábalos&Herreros
#059. *Vivienda y ciudad, avenida Diagonal*
Housing and the City competition, Avinguda Diagonal, Barcelona, 1989
AP164.S1.1989.D4.ARCH273287

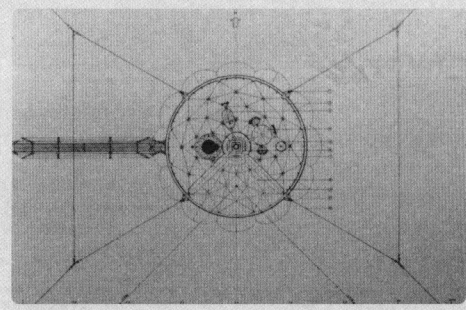

Future Systems
Project 117: Bubble, 1983
AP164.S3.D2.ARCH273087

Future Systems
Peanut, 1984
AP164.S3.D2.ARCH273089

Carpet

The exhibition includes a re-interpretation of the Gerhard Richter carpet that Ábalos&Herreros used in their design for the Third Biennial of Spanish Architecture and Urbanism in Comillas and Madrid, in 1996 and 1997.

View of Gerhard Richter's *1025 Farben* carpet,
From the *Farben* series, c. 1970
Ink-jet print on paper
AP164.S1.1995.D2.ARCH273283

Site panoramas

#075 *Puerto Málaga*
Port of Málaga, 1992

Photomontages of gelatin silver prints with pressure-sensitive tape
AP164.S1.1992.D1.ARCH272890, AP164.S1.1992.D1.ARCH272891

#083 *Ordenación del área de Abandoibarra*
Planning proposal for the Abandoibarra area, Bilbao, 1993

Collage of electrostatic prints and patterned drafting appliqué with marker, graphite and pen
AP164.S1.1993.D5.ARCH272910

#084 *Parque Dunar, Doñana*
Dune Park, Doñana National Park, 1993–1994

Photomontages of chromogenic prints with pressure-sensitive tape
AP164.S1.1993.D6.ARCH272900, AP164.S1.1993.D6.ARCH272901,
AP164.S1.1993.D6.ARCH272902

#099 *Planta de reciclaje de residuos urbanos de Valdemingómez*
Recycling plant for urban waste, Valdemingómez, Madrid, 1996–1999

Ink-jet print on photographic paper
AP164.S1.1996.D4.ARCH273197

#116 *Paseo marítimo Torrevieja*
Waterfront promenade, Torrevieja, 1999

Digital prints
AP164.S1.1999.D3.ARCH276132, AP164.S1.1999.D3.ARCH276131

#133 *Parque litoral Nord-est, Barcelona Forum 2004*
Nord-est coast park, Barcelona Forum 2004, 2000–2004

Photomontages of chromogenic prints with pressure-sensitive tape
AP164.S1.2000.D9.SD1.ARCH273204, AP164.S1.2000.D9.SD1.ARCH273203

#083. *Ordenación del área de Abandoibarra*
Planning proposal for the Abandoibarra area,
Bilbao, 1993
AP164.S1.1993.D5

#116. *Paseo marítimo Torrevieja*
Waterfront promenade, Torrevieja, 1999
AP164.S1.1999.D3

#133. *Parque litoral Nord-est, Barcelona Forum 2004*
Nord-est coast park, Barcelona Forum 2004, 2000–2004
AP164.S1.2000.D9.SD1

Collages

#075   *Puerto Málaga*
Port of Málaga, 1992

Collage of electrostatic prints with photo-offset lithography, pressure-sensitive tape and chromogenic prints
AP164.S1.1992.D1.ARCH273429

Collage of electrostatic prints with coloured pencil
AP164.S1.1992.D1.ARCH273428

#083   *Ordenación del área de Abandoibarra*
Planning proposal for the Abandoibarra area, Bilbao, 1993

Ink-jet print on paper
AP164.S1.1993.D5.ARCH273193

#084   *Parque Dunar, Doñana*
Dune Park, Doñana National Park, 1993–1994

Collage of electrostatic prints with white paint and black marker
AP164.S1.1993.D6.ARCH272905

Collage of electrophotographic prints
AP164.S1.1993.D6.ARCH272906

Collage of electrostatic prints with marker on paper
AP164.S1.1993.D6.ARCH272904

Collage of electrostatic prints with marker and graphite
AP164.S1.1993.D6.ARCH272907

#099   *Planta de reciclaje de residuos urbanos de Valdemingómez*
Recycling plant for urban waste, Valdemingómez, Madrid, 1996–1999

Collage of electrostatic prints and patterned drafting appliqué
AP164.S1.1996.D4.ARCH272894

Collage of electrostatic prints and coloured and patterned drafting appliqué
AP164.S1.1996.D4.ARCH272898

Collage of electrostatic prints, photo-offset lithographs and patterned drafting appliqué with marker, pressure-sensitive tape and white correction fluid
AP164.S1.1996.D4.ARCH271640

Collage of electrostatic prints with photo-offset lithograph, marker and graphite
AP164.S1.1996.D4.ARCH272895

#116   *Paseo marítimo Torrevieja*
Waterfront promenade, Torrevieja, 1999

Ink-jet print
AP164.S1.1999.D3.ARCH273517

Digital print
AP164.S1.1999.D3.ARCH276128

#133   *Parque litoral Nord-est, Barcelona Forum 2004*
Nord-est coast park, Barcelona Forum 2004, 2000–2004

Digital print
AP164.S1.2000.D9.SD1.ARCH276129

#084. *Parque Dunar, Doñana*
Dune Park, Doñana National Park, 1993–1994
AP164.S1.1993.D6

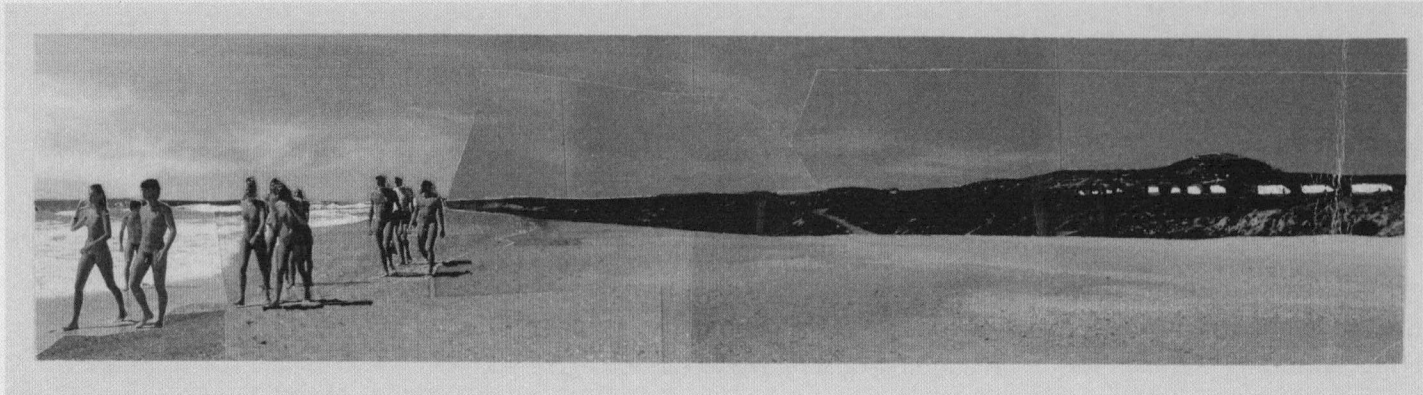

#084. *Parque Dunar, Doñana*
Dune Park, Doñana National Park, 1993–1994
AP164.S1.1993.D6

#099. *Planta de reciclaje de residuos urbanos de Valdemingómez*
Recycling plant for urban waste, Valdemingómez, Madrid, 1996–1999
AP164.S1.1996.D4

#084. *Parque Dunar, Doñana*
Dune Park, Doñana National Park, 1993–1994
AP164.S1.1993.D6

Site plans showing proposed developments

#075 *Puerto Málaga*
Port of Málaga, 1992

Plot (computer drawing) and pressure-sensitive tape
AP164.S1.1992.D1.ARCH273432

#083 *Ordenación del área de Abandoibarra*
Planning proposal for the Abandoibarra area, Bilbao, 1993

Print on photographic paper
AP164.S1.1993.D5.ARCH273192

#084 *Parque Dunar, Doñana*
Dune Park, Doñana National Park, 1993–1994

Graphite and coloured pencil on translucent paper overlaid on electrostatic print on paper
AP164.S1.1993.D6.ARCH273205

#099 *Planta de reciclaje de residuos urbanos de Valdemingómez*
Recycling plant for urban waste, Valdemingómez, Madrid, 1996–1999

Ink-jet print on paper
AP164.S1.1996.D4.ARCH273198

#116 *Paseo marítimo Torrevieja*
Waterfront promenade, Torrevieja, 1999

Electrostatic print on paper
AP164.S1.1999.D3.ARCH273200

#133 *Parque litoral Nord-est, Barcelona Forum 2004*
Nord-est coast park, Barcelona Forum 2004, 2000–2004

Digital print
AP164.S1.2000.D9.SD1.ARCH273196

Landscapes of the Hyperreal
Florian Idenburg and Jing Liu

Ábalos&Herreros constructed landscapes—or, more precisely, assembled them—by crudely juxtaposing a cast of semi-familiar characters. Novel to Spanish architecture in the 1980s, this pragmatic method of appropriation was developed and consistently employed as part of a design process. Borrowing, incorporating and transforming allowed Ábalos&Herreros to absorb the modernist canon, and to introduce a wide variety of architectural and visual-art references. Their language of assemblage is vivid, dynamic and non-dogmatic. The collage here is not only a form of representation, but also a means of production.

    Ábalos&Herreros developed landscape projects in areas that had remained largely out of view. This new, liberated landscape—a direct result of the socio-economic conditions that were shaping Spain following the end of the Franco regime—shifted attention from the centre to the periphery. They actively chose to redefine these sites and to make them subjects of concern for the architect. These new programmatic interests included waste and recycling centres, sports and (nudist) recreation sites, ports, highways and airports. Through a process of appropriation, Ábalos& Herreros generated a number of architectural characters: the shed, the double tower, the environmental structure, the machinic device and the pattern. They introduced these characters again and again in various proposals to populate, animate and activate new contexts, from the derelict industrial harbour of Bilbao to the undeveloped rural area of Valdemingómez.

    The characters, initially siteless and "pure," start to coalesce; the soup gets thicker and murkier and the resolution intensifies. No longer able to operate autonomously, the landscape becomes an interrelated system, a hyperreal synthesis of the natural and the artificial. It is a new nature, made an integral part of the architectural proposition.

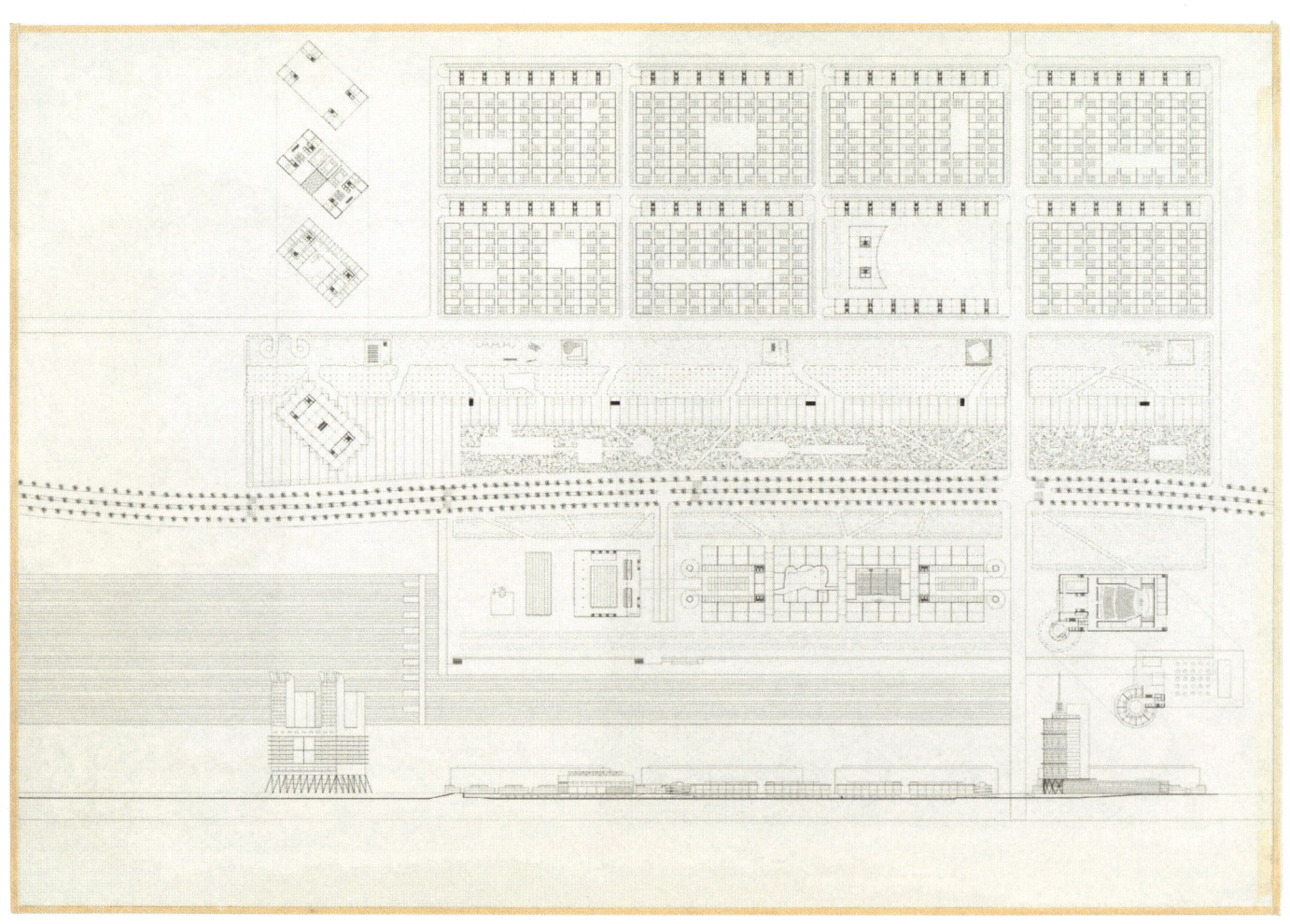

Opposite, top: Site panorama for the port of Málaga, 1992. Photomontage of gelatin silver prints and pressure-sensitive tape, 11.1 × 53 cm. AP164.S1.1992.D1.ARCH272890

Opposite, bottom: Site plan for the port of Málaga, 1992. Plot (computer drawing) and pressure-sensitive tape, 71.4 × 105.9 cm. AP164.S1.1992.D1.ARCH273432

Above: Collage for the port of Málaga, 1992. Electrostatic prints with photo-offset lithography, pressure-sensitive tape and chromogenic prints, 32.6 × 38.9 cm. AP164.S1.1992.D1.ARCH273429

Florian Idenburg and Jing Liu

Opposite, top: Site panorama for the plan for the Abandoibarra area of Bilbao, 1993. Collage of electrostatic prints and patterned drafting appliqué with marker, graphite and pen, 22.5 × 81.6 cm. AP164.S1.1993.D5.ARCH272910

Opposite, bottom: Collage for the plan for the Abandoibarra area of Bilbao, 1993. Ink-jet print on paper, 32.4 × 32.7 cm. AP164.S1.1993.D5.ARCH273193

Top: Site panorama for Dune Park, Doñana National Park, c. 1993–1994. Photomontage of chromogenic prints with pressure-sensitive tape, 12.1 × 59.5 cm. AP164.S1.1993.D6.ARCH272902

Above: Collage for Dune Park, Doñana National Park, c. 1993–1994. Electrostatic prints with white paint and black marker, 7.5 × 31.3 cm. AP164.S1.1993.D6.ARCH272905

Florian Idenburg and Jing Liu

179

Opposite: Collage for Dune Park, Doñana National Park, c. 1993–1994. Electrostatic prints with marker and graphite, 15.9 × 36.4 cm. AP164.S1.1993.D6.ARCH272907

Above: Collage for Dune Park, Doñana National Park, c. 1993–1994. Electrophotographic prints, 16.2 × 28.7 cm. AP164.S1.1993.D6.ARCH27290

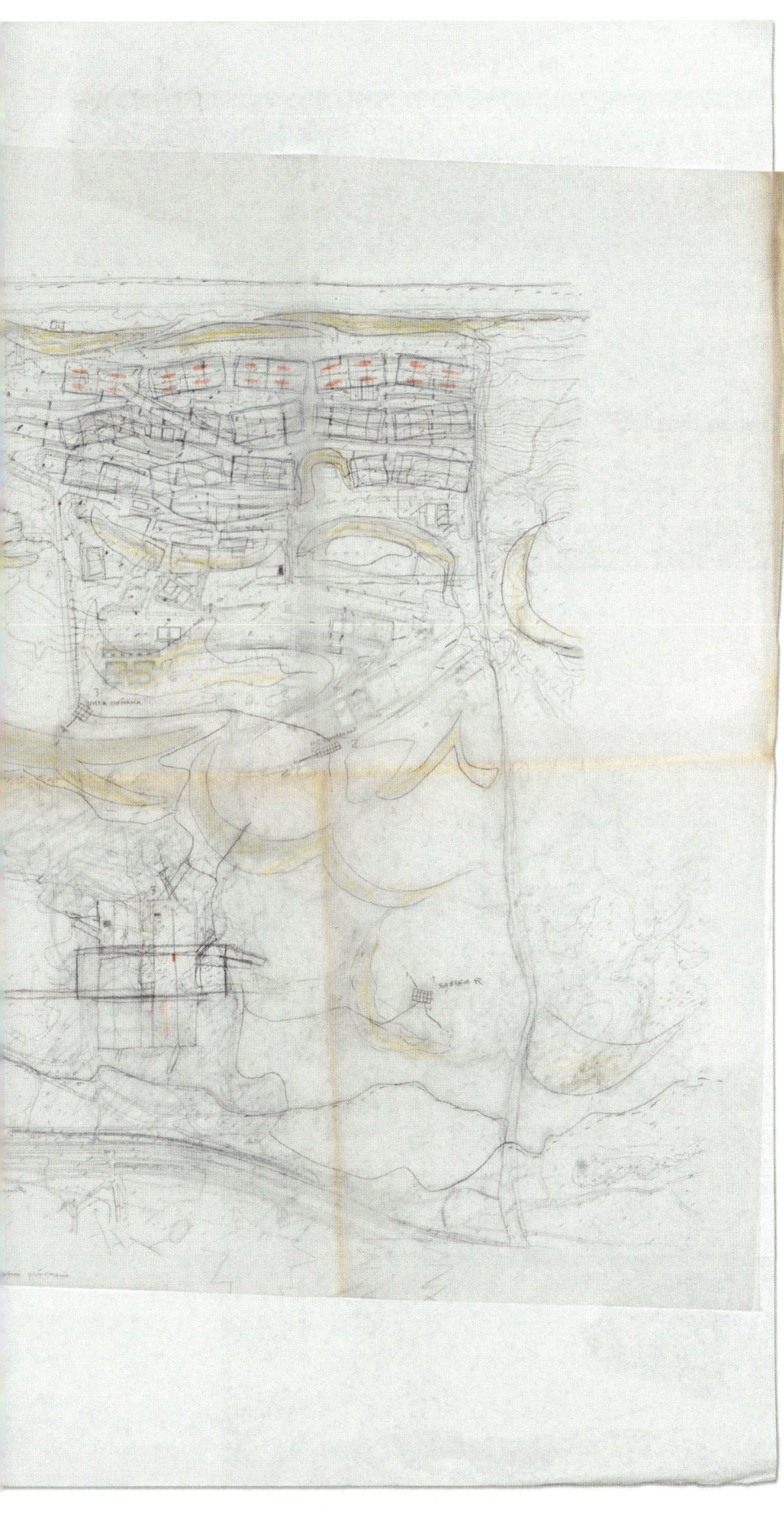

Site plan for Dune Park, Doñana
National Park, c. 1993–1994.
Graphite and coloured
pencil on translucent paper
overlaid on an electrostatic
print on paper, 90 × 106.8 cm.
AP164.S1.1993.D6.ARCH273205

Opposite, top: Collage for the recycling plant for urban waste, Valdemingómez, c. 1996–1999. Electrostatic prints and patterned drafting appliqué with marker, graphite and pen, 13.3 × 35.6 cm. AP164.S1.1996.D4.ARCH272894

Opposite, bottom: Collage for the recycling plant for urban waste, Valdemingómez, c. 1996–1999. Electrostatic prints with photo-offset lithograph, marker and graphite, 24.8 × 31.1 cm. AP164.S1.1996.D4.ARCH272895

Top: Site panorama for the waterfront promenade, Torrevieja, 1999. Digital image. AP164.S1.1999.D3.ARCH276132

Above: Collage for the waterfront promenade, Torrevieja, 1999. Digital image. AP164.S1.1999.D3.ARCH276128

Florian Idenburg and Jing Liu

Above: Collage for the waterfront promenade, Torrevieja, 1999. Ink-jet print, 21 × 29.7 cm. AP164.S1.1999.D3.ARCH27351

Opposite: Site panorama for the Nord-est coast park, Barcelona Forum 2004, c. 2000–2004. Photomontage of chromogenic prints and pressure-sensitive tape, 29.5 × 44.8 cm. AP164.S1.2000.D9.ARCH273204

Florian Idenburg and Jing Liu

Top: Site panorama for the Nord-est coast park, Barcelona Forum 2004, c. 2000–2004. Photomontage of chromogenic prints and pressure-sensitive tape, 24.5 × 82.6 cm. AP164.S1.2000.D9.ARCH273203

Above: Collage for the Nord-est coast park, Barcelona Forum 2004, c. 2000–2004. Digital image. AP164.S1.2000.D9.ARCH276129

July 2015

Florian Idenburg and Jing Liu unpack their research methodology and curatorial strategy. Comments by Iñaki Ábalos and Juan Herreros appear in red.

• Iñaki Ábalos: Working together was a way of being a collage. We have different backgrounds, even if at one point they thought we were brothers, because we were really similar physically. We were working at a table constantly.

Juan Herreros: At the same table.

IA: We put different things together on the table and tried to merge them, or to force them to contrast.

JH: Our working method was based on dialogue, discussion and exchange of ideas. This was a very productive way of forming new ideas that one of us never could have had by himself.
 Our pragmatism is not only theoretical. We were looking for opportunities to work in a new way and to develop proposals while playing with the rules of the game and being part of the system, with legal documents, regulations and clients.

•• IA: Terms related to velocity absolutely capture our method. Our technique allowed hyperreal things to be approached at such a speed that there is no need for explanation.

••• IA: Like many studios that are young and modest (in economic terms), we needed to produce content with minimal effort and cost. But the collages—which are basically traditional, in the sense of the modernist collage—are more than just a visualization of ideas. They explain concepts and form consistency by putting things together.
 The typological research is a combination of historical and contemporary types. Using the catalogue is a way to appropriate the knowledge and talent of others to produce something new.

Florian Idenburg: We are neither historians, nor scholars nor researchers; we are practising architects. In this research and exhibition project we are exploring the relationship between two sets of practising architects. The other two curators in the series of exhibitions have a more intimate connection to Ábalos&Herreros than we have. When I was a student, I learned about the work of Ábalos&Herreros only through Actar's publications. So Jing and I were open-minded when we began this project. Our initial impulse was to look at process and method, and at the dialogue that existed between Iñaki and Juan. It seemed that their work was generated through conversation, and we had the impression that the dialogue was active, energetic and volatile.

•
 We wanted to introduce into the exhibition the energy and the speed that we saw in the practice of Ábalos& Herreros. We quickly learned the difference between the practising architect and the scholar. It was interesting for us to work at a different pace, with the different kind of energy that comes with archival research.

••
Jing Liu: At first we were anxious because everything moved so slowly. We had to wear gloves in the archive and put back everything we took out in exactly the same way.
 In our own practice, we work at a fast pace with drawings, collages and sketches. Encountering this kind of material in the archive in such a restrained manner emphasized even more the speed at which content was created. Ábalos&Herreros developed a pragmatic approach and quickly appropriated architectural discourses and characters. They made liberal use of elements that appeared in historical contexts and incorporated them into their own projects. The reference material included in the exhibition frames these architectural appropriations.

FI: In the archive I was drawn to the building blocks with which they created their architectural language and narratives. I tried to identify the strands of architectural history that they used to build this cast of characters. Certain elements reappear, often transformed, over time in different projects.

•••
 We distilled five characters from the work of Ábalos&Herreros and from their teaching slides and reference materials. One character is the shed or the industrial box, an element that they used many times in these landscape projects. Another is the environmental structure or the structural experiment, which builds on Cedric Price's aviary and on Robert Le Ricolais, a structural engineer whose work fascinated them. Next is the double tower, which takes its cue from the cathedral of Notre-Dame but also from the co-ops on Central Park West and from Marina City. Then there is the machinic device, which is something at the scale of furniture: a high-tech concoction that is able to do anything. It represents technology and the computer. Finally, there is the graphic

01–02

IA: I think that the characters have a chronological order. I would say the shed is the first.

The shed and the machine are closely connected in terms of the technological facilities that we explored in our teaching, but we were hardly ever able to apply these characters. The double tower resulted from our interest in the skyscraper, but not in the infinite growth that the skyscraper often connotes. It shows that skyscrapers can be small and squat. The pattern comes from our interest in ornament and in art practices. The environmental structure resulted from our interest in landscape, nature and the picturesque.

JH: Perhaps because we studied the skyscraper in such depth, we were interested neither in the continuous floor plan nor in the continuous section, but rather in the richness of the double tower in terms of hybridization, in terms of the accumulation of different programs and in terms of a reconfiguration of the way of touching the ground.

pattern, which is something that gradually emerges and becomes more prominent across the projects that we selected.

•

JL: I was especially interested in a series of panoramic site photographs that Ábalos&Herreros took when they began work on a project and entered new, uncharted territories for architecture.

••

In Spain following the end of the Franco regime, there was a sense of urgency to find a new architectural language, which galvanized the field. Ábalos&Herreros went to the edges of cities to design projects for waste treatment plants and nudist beaches. These programs were sometimes defined by Ábalos&Herreros themselves, and sometimes they were given. But in all cases the peripheral territories had not been part of the architectural context before. It is easy to imagine how daunting it must have been for an architect to be thrown into this context and charged with defining architecture's position there.

In essence, these site pictures are photomontages. Rather than taking a single photograph from a distance, Ábalos&Herreros moved closer and pieced the images together at a scale that is larger than a single camera frame. They started to work on this landscape through the fast method of collage, and many of the pictures date from the pre-digital era. Ábalos&Herreros cut out car advertisements, for example— many American motifs are present—and then photocopied them over and over again. There are probably fifteen versions of these collages in the archive, which suggests that the working process was fast and energetic.

•••

We began to notice that the five characters we identified are the seeds for the energy in this emptiness, and are the first examples of something new injected into the landscapes. The characters and the landscapes came together in the six projects that we chose to feature in the exhibition. Obviously there are other projects that we did not select, but these six are quite representative of a span of about ten years of the work of Ábalos&Herreros.

FI: The projects we chose date from 1990 through 2000, although in fact the last project was realized in 2004. A shift is evident in these six projects: the Málaga harbour project, the Bilbao urban plan, the nudist beach in Doñana National Park, the recycling plant outside Madrid, the port of Torrevieja and the Nord-est coast park in Barcelona. In the earlier projects the characters and the landscapes seem disconnected; they gradually become

Fig. 01: Site panorama for Dune Park, Doñana National Park, c. 1993–1994. Photomontage of chromogenic prints with pressure-sensitive tape, 11.6 × 67.8. AP164.S1.1993.D6.ARCH272901 /
Fig. 02: Site panorama for Dune Park, Doñana National Park, c. 1993–1994. Photomontage of chromogenic prints with pressure-sensitive tape, 12.1 × 65.6 cm. AP164.S1.1993.D6.ARCH272900

•• JH: These site photographs are a realistic expression of how, in a changing Spain, our generation was expulsed from the city to work in the periphery. We attempted to transform the periphery into an interesting field of work. I am not sure we succeeded; in the end the periphery became something very different from our plans. But for us it was full of poetic opportunities for work, even if the photographs make it look like just a collection of disparate landscapes.

••• IA: I was particularly fascinated with the American cultural environment. In those days, Europe was boring and affirmative. All the doctrines—they were doctrines—were affirmative. American debates—not doctrines, but debates—were speculative, and I naturally felt a connection with the American media.

more integrated and synthetic. This development is connected to the emergence of the digital and the way in which the computer increased the resolution of the process, beginning in the mid-1990s.

But sometimes we were not able to date the projects that we encountered in the archive. For example, we saw a drawing that illustrates a project that happened more than once. One instance is at a harbour and one is near an airport, but the drawings are more or less the same. This could relate to the use of the computer, which Ábalos&Herreros had just bought at the time. They only knew how to copy and paste and to array.

JL: And it is clear that they eventually also learned how to rotate objects on the computer.

In the gallery we installed a carpet, which is a reference to a Gerhard Richter carpet that Ábalos&Herreros used in the Third Biennial of Spanish Architecture and Urbanism in 1996 and 1997. But we chose the carpet's colours. We wanted to give the visitor a tactile experience that is connected to the artificiality of the landscapes that Ábalos&Herreros created in the new peripheral areas.

FI: We wanted to create a panorama in the way Ábalos&Herreros saw the new landscape. The exhibition as a landscape was an undercurrent in our thinking. We did not want to do a scholarly, systematic show, but rather an experiential one that would resemble an immersion in the archive. If this were a large show that included many different works, it would probably be useful to provide more explanation. But the exhibition consists of one room and essentially makes a single point: the artificiality of the landscape.

The reality of the practice of Ábalos&Herreros became apparent as we looked through the material; the strategy of making do with what you have was especially clear. This is an aspect of the work that could easily be overlooked if the material is not approached with a practitioner's perspective. The tools are very present in the archive.

Ábalos&Herreros were skilled at creating new stories. By encountering these new landscapes and developing this cast of characters through collages, they projected new kinds of architectural experiences. We are interested in fiction, artificiality and the subjective narrative as ways to generate an architecture.

There is something of assembly and of improvisation in this way of working that resonates with me. Ábalos&Herreros were interested in leaving Spain to become international architects, which is similar to what was happening at SANAA in Japan when I was there. The idea of being an international practice is also something with which Jing and I feel an affinity.

03

Fig. 03: Site panorama for the waterfront promenade, Torrevieja, 1999. Digital image. AP164.S1.1999.D3.ARCH276131

Iñaki is my boss at the GSD, and Juan is Jing's boss at Columbia. Jing and I made a rule for ourselves that we would not ask Juan and Iñaki anything about the material in the archive. Last semester Iñaki organized an exhibition at the GSD of work from his current practice; the landscape is present in his exhibition and in this one. Iñaki's show prominently featured a project for the railway station in Logroño, which has a large park at the top. Elements like this were crudely collaged in the earlier years of Ábalos&Herreros's practice and became more synthetic over time. Structure and nature, the artificial and the natural, begin to merge, and Iñaki is continuing in this direction in his work with Renata Sentkiewicz.

Iñaki's show included some older models that had been relabelled to create a new narrative: a reappropriation of his own archive to form a new story. The technique of creating new narratives continues to be one of his strengths.

JL: And Juan did an exhibition of his work at the Architecture Biennale in Venice in 2012. It was very much about collaboration and the conversation between architects, consultants, clients and city officials. This emphasis on context is also apparent in the work of Ábalos&Herreros.

There are many practitioners who teach these days, but many people just juggle the two activities and do not think seriously about the synthesis. Working at Columbia, I am struck by Juan's teaching. The connection with history and with the younger generation is an important aspect of both the teaching and the design work of Ábalos&Herreros, as well. The way they integrated teaching into their practice showed me that the two activities can be a single project.

But some of the material we found in the archive did not correspond to the Ábalos&Herreros we knew. During our first few days, we found only dry documents: texts, hard-line drawings, construction drawings and spec books. We thought that Ábalos&Herreros were constantly on the go: on bicycles, walking, on the subway, and unconcerned with technical documents. It was only later that we opened a box and found a collage.

FI: We were looking for energy, but we initially found only texts and legal documents. We were projecting what we hoped to find onto the material.

04–05

Fig. 04: Gerhard Richter. Colour sample for a carpet commission, 1995. Colour slide, 5 × 5 cm. AP164.S3.D2.ARCH273069 / Fig. 05: View of Gerhard Richter's *1025 Farben* carpet. From the *Farben* series, c. 1970. Ink-jet print on paper, 29.7 × 21 cm. AP164.S1.1995.D2.ARCH273283

06

• JH: In those years, it was common practice for every drawing to be done twice: one version is the sketch and the other is the ink production. But we wanted to make both versions at the same time that we were thinking them. The archive has about twenty versions of each collage. The collage was fast so it could accompany the thinking process. It is both a sketch and a final drawing. The idea that the process is also the way of producing the definitive thing was important for our way of working.

JL: We were looking for study models in the archive, because in our office we have so many models. But basically there are no models here. This made us see even more clearly the fast pace at which they worked. Their process is very different from our own, and we saw this contrast only after we came to the archive.

•

FI: For the most part, Ábalos&Herreros did not use models. They insisted that if a model is needed to explain the project, then the project is probably too difficult to build.

They had an interest in plastics and other new materials. This introduction of untrue materials was happening at SANAA at the same time. It is an aspect of their work that we did not include in the exhibition, but the archive contains seemingly endless catalogues of meshes, of plastics and of polycarbonates. One of their early projects north of Madrid is essentially a shed with corrugated plastic siding. Ábalos&Herreros were highly skilled architects with these simple materials.

This research made us think seriously about archiving, and about how we archive our own material. I still think that we are an office that just started, although this is our eighth year. There is no time for reflection in the beginning. Our research on Ábalos&Herreros gave us a distance that allowed us to think in the long term about our own practice.

I realized to what extent the work of Ábalos&Herreros is part of a certain era, namely the last decade of the last century. This was the time of European unification: a neo-liberal period of globalization, the withdrawal of the State and the emergence of the computer. I think their work could have only been produced at this time. This led us to notice the architecture that is of our own time and to see the recycling of ideas. There is a body of knowledge that we can use as the discipline moves forward.

JL: We should also mention the digital material. The digital archive of Ábalos&Herreros was quite messy, as any early digital archive would be. We started opening files and we realized that this raises many new questions.

Fig. 06: Photograph of an installation in Comillas in 1996, designed by Ábalos&Herreros for the Third Biennial of Spanish Architecture and Urbanism, showing viewing devices and the Gerhard Richter carpet. 12.9 × 19.3 cm. AP164.S1.1995.D2.ARCH273101

Florian Idenburg and Jing Liu

07

FI: We first looked through the physical material because we were interested in the mode in which Ábalos&Herreros developed their language, which happened before the computer. It was only toward the end of our research that we investigated the digital material. Many of the patterns are digital, but we mostly articulated our point through the physical panoramas and collages. Site panoramas give insight into the period during which Ábalos&Herreros first went to the periphery and realized that it was fertile land. It was a liberation from the city and from the method of architectural production connected to an urban context. In addition to being new land, the periphery allowed for a new method.

JL: I was recently in Barcelona, and at the site of the Barcelona Forum 2004 as well as within the city, architects and officials are trying to solve problems created by the most recent financial crisis. It is important to note that the current situation in Spain is very different from the Spain of the 1990s. Ábalos& Herreros were not trying to fix an existing situation; they were trying to create something new.

FI: But very few of these projects were built. The Nord-est coast park in Barcelona was completed, but it was not maintained and it already looks derelict. The landscape projects of Ábalos& Herreros are more of a promise than something that was actually realized.

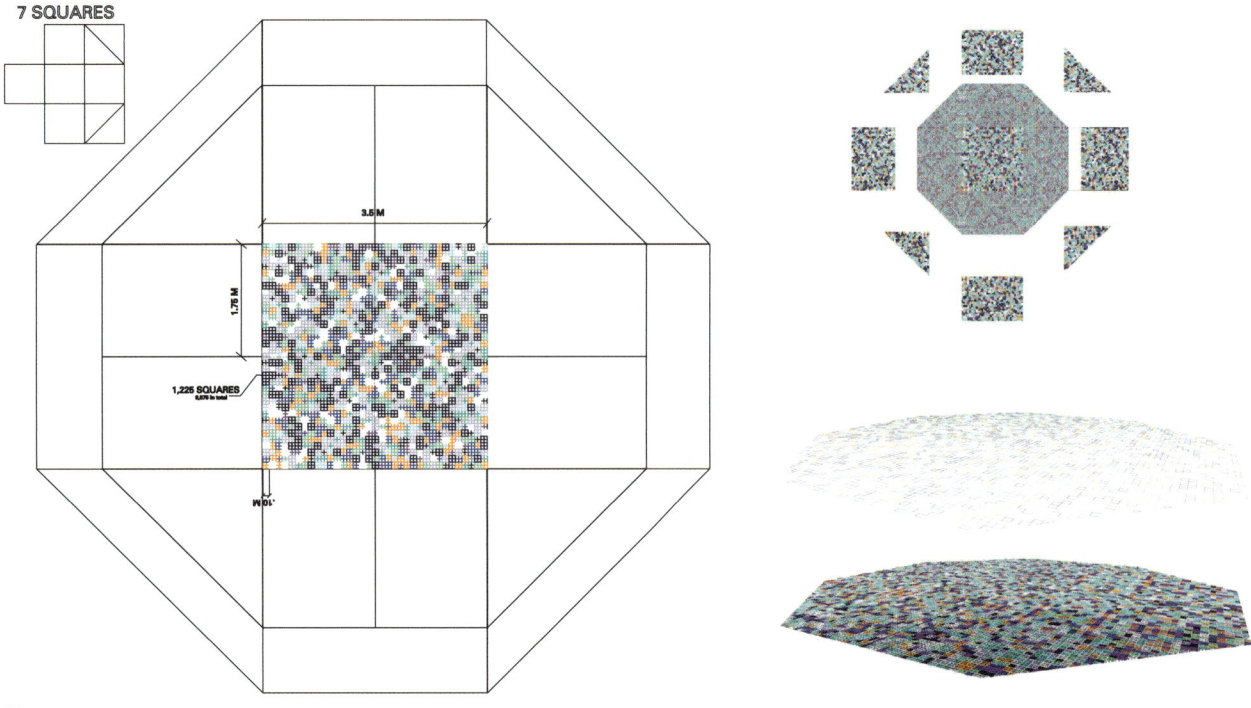

08

Fig. 07: Installation view showing the carpet with a pattern designed by Florian Idenburg and Jing Liu / Fig. 08: Design concept for a carpet, by Florian Idenburg and Jing Liu

A decade has gone by since Ábalos & Herreros disappeared. It ceased to exist when it was in danger of becoming a burden rather than continuing to be an incentive for creativity and personal freedom.

I have often repeated this obvious fact, and just how aware we both were that constructing separate voices was going to take a lot of work. But that paled into insignificance beside our greatest motivation: how to continue growing as architects and avoid the pitfalls of inertia.

Seeing the three exhibitions and their curators' different projections of the architecture we produced together, I feel gratified that the subjects which were important to us then continue to convey their vitality to the younger generations, and that we were right in our diagnosis and the radical remedy we adopted during twenty years of Ábalos & Herreros.

Today, brilliant architects who spent time at our studio have developed careers with the vigour and radicality that we promoted and, like us, both then and now, they combine academic and professional work as the natural expression of being an architect.

Nothing could make me happier than seeing the productivity of the years of Ábalos & Herreros in the gallery at the CCA, through the eyes of some of the people currently at the forefront of young European and American architecture. It is gratifying to see the effect that a clean legacy, with no second-class interventions and no dark corners, may have had on them.

The generous reception by the CCA of our body of work is marvellous confirmation that integrity is an architect's most valuable asset.

Iñaki Ábalos
September 2015

From the twenty years of Ábalos & Herreros, I'll take the cavalier optimism that allowed us to be incisive and freed us from the strict rules that limited the practice and teaching of architecture in the Spain of the 1980s. It meant that the cult of context, reverence for composition based on well-defined volumes and respect for the modern classics bordering on mythomania gave way to other ways of seeing and acting. Context became information, design composition and organization sought out experimental connections with new technologies and materiality, and history, recent and remote, became a fabulous legacy that allowed for experiment and appropriation.

It was over the course of those years that I understood something that is now fundamental to my way of practising and teaching architecture: each project must distil its own working system, its own references and its own discourse. This experimental approach has nothing to do with turning your back on models, but rather addresses the capacity to construct a new syntax based on known materials and ideas that are reorganized instantaneously and differently in each case. This reorganization of what is available is the intellectual condition by means of which architecture anchors itself to its time and offers glimpses of a possible future.

Ábalos & Herreros is now in the past and therefore it is material available to anyone who wishes to use it to explore the present. The three interpretations included in this book are examples of the utility for other admired colleagues of a legacy that is free of self-absorption. The dialogue that emerges from three different gazes inspires my appreciation for the twenty years and my thanks to the authors for bringing it to light.

Juan Herreros
September 2015

The Ábalos&Herreros archive began to be organized and catalogued over the course of the three research residencies. A description of the archive's structure and a list of projects are presented here.

Archives privées 164, or AP164, denotes the Ábalos&Herreros archive at the CCA.

The archive documents the activities of the architects Iñaki Ábalos and Juan Herreros over the course of the firm's existence from 1985 until 2008. It also provides a record of their writing, teaching, curating and research. The archive consists primarily of photographic material and drawings done for design and concept development, presentation, exhibition and publication, and also contains textual records, models and digital material.

Ábalos&Herreros's work began in Madrid, where they maintained their office. Projects were developed for the periphery of the city, and the firm expanded its work to projects for sites elsewhere in Spain, Europe and the Americas.

The firm's design activities encompass residential, government, commercial, transportation and urban-planning projects, as well as projects for mixed-use buildings, waste-management facilities, sports centres, educational institutions and parks.

The archive includes over 16,000 photographic materials, approximately 6,000 drawings, and over 5 linear metres of textual records. It also contains models, collages, floppy disks, DVDs and maps.

AP164 is arranged according to three series: Architectural Projects; Exhibitions, Teaching and Writing; and Office Documentation.

S1: Architectural Projects
This series documents Ábalos&Herreros's architectural projects, which range from commercial, residential, urban-planning and landscape-architecture projects to projects for civic buildings, sports and recreation centres, art galleries, educational institutions and industrial buildings.

Several projects were developed in collaboration with other architects, including José Manuel Ábalos, Salvador Pérez Arroyo, Filippo Costi, Ángel Jaramillo Esteban, Javier Fresneda, Eduardo Horta, Martín Marciano, Ángel Jaramillo Sánchez, Renata Sentkiewicz and Héctor Vigliecca.

Projects were developed for the Madrid region, as well as for other sites in Spain, including the Canary Islands, and for sites in Portugal, Germany, the United States and Brazil.

Project dates range from 1986 through 2006.

S2: Exhibitions, Teaching and Writing
This series documents the curatorial, teaching and writing activities of Iñaki Ábalos and Juan Herreros, and of their firm, Ábalos&Herreros.

Material was produced between 1986 and 2006, and is arranged according to four categories: exhibitions, lectures, writings and teaching.

S3: Office Documentation
This series contains Ábalos&Herreros's office documentation, including portfolios, curricula vitae, textual records and photographic material. Photographs were used as reference for projects and lectures.

The dates of the activities range from 1977 through 2006. The series is arranged according to document type: promotional materials and photographic materials.

Project	Nr.	Spanish title	English title	Location
AP164.S1.1986.D1	39	Polideportivo y piscina cubierta de Vallecas	Sports hall and indoor swimming pool	Vallecas, Madrid, Spain
AP164.S1.1986.D2	36	Ordenación de la Plaza Mayor, Villamantilla	Planning proposal for Plaza Mayor	Villamantilla, Madrid, Spain
AP164.S1.1986.D3	37	Ordenación de la Plaza del Marqués de Mamblas, Sevilla la Nueva	Planning proposal for Plaza del Marqués de Mamblas	Sevilla la Nueva, Madrid, Spain
AP164.S1.1986.D4	38	Centro cultural, Cobeña	Cobeña cultural center	Cobeña, Spain
AP164.S1.1986.D5	40	Tres depuradoras de aguas residuales: Villalba, Guadarrama, Majadahonda	Three waste-water treatment plants	Villalba, Guadarrama and Majadahonda, Madrid, Spain
AP164.S1.1986.D5.SD1	40.1	Estación depuradora de aguas residuales "El Endrinal," Villalba	El Endrinal waste-water treatment plant	Collado-Villalba, Spain
AP164.S1.1986.D5.SD2	40.2	Estación depuradora de aguas residuales, Majadahonda	Waste-water treatment plant	Majadahonda, Madrid, Spain
AP164.S1.1986.D5.SD3	40.3	Estación depuradora de aguas residuales "El Chaparral," Guadarrama	El Chaparral waste-water treatment plant	Guadarrama, Madrid, Spain
AP164.S1.1986.D6	42	Ordenación de la Plaza de Castilla	Planning proposal for Plaza de Castilla	Madrid, Spain
AP164.S1.1986.D7	43	Soluciones sobre nuevas tecnologías de vivienda social	New technologies for social housing	
AP164.S1.1986.D8	44	Prototipo de vivienda de madera	Prototype for a house made of wood	
AP164.S1.1987.D1	45	Ordenación de Nueva Montaña Quijano en Santander	Planning proposal for Nueva Montaña Quijano	Santander, Spain
AP164.S1.1987.D2	46	Ordenación del nudo Puerta de Hierro	Planning proposal for the Puerta de Hierro intersection	Madrid, Spain
AP164.S1.1987.D3	48	Prototipo de estructura vertical	Prototype for a vertical structure	Cáceres, Spain
AP164.S1.1988.D1	47	Casa Andradas		San Lorenzo del Escorial, Spain
AP164.S1.1988.D2	49	Sistema constructivo Jonas	Jonas construction system	
AP164.S1.1988.D3	50	Viviendas, locales y garajes en la M-30	Housing, commercial units and garages on the M-30	Madrid, Spain
AP164.S1.1988.D4	51	Propuesta para la Plaza de Ópera	Proposal for the Plaza de Ópera	Madrid, Spain
AP164.S1.1988.D5	52	Parque de las Naciones		Madrid, Spain
AP164.S1.1988.D6	53	Iglesia María Auxiliadora, Lomé	María Auxiliadora church	Lomé, Togo
AP164.S1.1988.D7	54	Polígono industrial Alcorcón	Alcorcón industrial park	Alcorcón, Spain
AP164.S1.1988.D8	55	Estantería	Shelving	
AP164.S1.1989.D1	56	Centro de cálculo de Telefónica	Data centre for Telefónica	Madrid, Spain
AP164.S1.1989.D2	57	Cantones de Isabel II		Torrelodones, Spain
AP164.S1.1989.D3	58	Edificio de oficinas de RENFE	RENFE office building	Madrid, Spain
AP164.S1.1989.D4	59	Vivienda y ciudad, avenida Diagonal, Barcelona	Housing and the City competition, Avinguda Diagonal	Barcelona, Spain
AP164.S1.1989.D5	60	Adecuación del canódromo de Carabanchel para velódromo	Conversion of the Carabanchel dog track into a velodrome	Madrid, Spain
AP164.S1.1989.D6	61	Achna, cierre y pérgolas de acceso	ACHNA fencing and access pergola	Madrid, Spain
AP164.S1.1990.D1	62	Polideportivo los Zumacales	Los Zumacales sports hall	Simancas, Spain
AP164.S1.1990.D2	63	Polideportivo Parquesol	Parquesol sports hall	Valladolid, Spain
AP164.S1.1990.D3	64	Edificio administrativo para el Ministerio del Interior	Administrative building for the Ministry of the Interior	Madrid, Spain
AP164.S1.1990.D4	65	RENFE Burgos		Burgos, Spain
AP164.S1.1990.D5	66	VIPS Arturo Soria		Madrid, Spain
AP164.S1.1990.D6	67	Polideportivo Madrigal de las Altas Torres	Sports hall	Madrigal de las Altas Torres, Ávila, Spain
AP164.S1.1990.D7	68	City VIPS, Fuencarral		Fuencarral, Madrid, Spain
AP164.S1.1990.D8	70	Grassy, reforma de locales	Renovation proposal, Grassy	Madrid, Spain
AP164.S1.1991.D1	71	Concurso Embajada de Francia	Embassy of France competition	Madrid, Spain
AP164.S1.1991.D2	72	Palencia Parque Europa	Europa Park	Palencia, Spain
AP164.S1.1991.D3	73	Madrid Sur		Madrid, Spain
AP164.S1.1991.D4	74	Galería de Arte Castello		Madrid, Spain
AP164.S1.1992.D1	75	Puerto Málaga	Port of Málaga	Málaga, Spain
AP164.S1.1992.D2	76	Ayuntamiento y casa de la cultura de Cobeña	Town hall and cultural centre	Cobeña, Spain
AP164.S1.1992.D3	77	Centro cívico y comercial, Majadahonda	Commercial and civic centre	Majadahonda, Madrid, Spain
AP164.S1.1992.D4	78	Caja de Ahorros de Granada	Head office for the Savings Bank of Granada	Granada, Spain
AP164.S1.1993.D1	79	Casa Urbasos		Madrid, Spain
AP164.S1.1993.D2	80	Casa Gordillo		Villanueva de la Cañada, Spain
AP164.S1.1993.D3	81	Casa Blanco		El Escorial, Madrid, Spain
AP164.S1.1993.D4	82	Encauzamiento del río Guadalhorce	Channelling of the Guadalhorce River	Málaga, Spain
AP164.S1.1993.D5	83	Ordenación del área de Abandoibarra, Bilbao	Planning proposal for the Abandoibarra area	Bilbao, Spain
AP164.S1.1993.D6	84	Parque Dunar, Doñana	Dune Park	Doñana National Park, Spain
AP164.S1.1993.D7	85	Unidad residencial de Barajas	Housing block	Barajas, Madrid, Spain

Project	Nr.	Spanish title	English title	Location
AP164.S1.1993.D8	86	Bacaladera		Irun, Spain
AP164.S1.1993.D9	87	Saconia		Madrid, Spain
AP164.S1.1993.D10	88	Vivienda social (concurso)	Social housing (competition)	Madrid, Spain
AP164.S1.1993.D11	89	Prototipos de vivienda industrializada: Casas AH-Gia	Industrialized housing prototypes: AH-Gia Houses	
AP164.S1.1994.D1	90	IKEA Alcorcón		Alcorcón, Spain
AP164.S1.1994.D2	91	Concurso Zephyr: torres mixtas autosuficientes	Zephyr Competition: self-sufficient hybrid towers	Madrid, Spain
AP164.S1.1994.D3	93	Moscú	Moscow	Moscow, Russia
AP164.S1.1995.D1	94	Biblioteca de Usera	Usera library	Madrid, Spain
AP164.S1.1995.D2	95	III Bienal Arquitectura Española	Third Biennial of Spanish Architecture and Urbanism	Comillas and Madrid, Spain
AP164.S1.1996.D1	96	Universitat Pompeu Fabra, edificio departamental y aulario	Department building and classrooms, Pompeu Fabra University	Barcelona, Spain
AP164.S1.1996.D2	97	Centro cívico Alcobendas	Civic centre	Alcobendas, Madrid, Spain
AP164.S1.1996.D3	98	Facultad de filosofía y ciencias de la educación, Cáceres	Faculty of Philosophy and Education Science	Cáceres, Spain
AP164.S1.1996.D4	99	Planta de reciclaje de residuos urbanos de Valdemingómez	Recycling plant for urban waste	Valdemingómez, Madrid, Spain
AP164.S1.1997.D1	100	Centro Flassaders en Palma de Mallorca	Centre Flassaders	Palma de Mallorca, Spain
AP164.S1.1997.D2	101	Centro interactivo y ecomuseo de La Cabrera	Interactive centre and eco-museum	La Cabrera, Madrid, Spain
AP164.S1.1997.D3	102	La Casa del Presidente	The President's House	
AP164.S1.1997.D4	103	Casa Verde		Pozuelo de Alarcón, Madrid, Spain
AP164.S1.1997.D5	104	Casa González		Madrid, Spain
AP164.S1.1997.D6	105	Casa en La Moraleja	House in La Moraleja	Alcobendas, Madrid, Spain
AP164.S1.1997.D7	106	Recualificación del espacio público de Ramos	Planning proposal for public space	Ramos, Rio de Janeiro, Brazil
AP164.S1.1997.D8	107	Delegación de hacienda, Almería	Tax office	Almería, Spain
AP164.S1.1997.D9	108	Architekturforum Bonn		Bonn, Germany
AP164.S1.1997.D10	109	Biblioteca Central Campus Cáceres	Central campus library	Cáceres, Spain
AP164.S1.1997.D11	112	Sala municipal y plaza en Colmenarejo	City hall and main square	Colmenarejo, Spain
AP164.S1.1998.D1	111	Centro de control y aula medioambiental de Arico	Environmental education centre and offices	Arico, Tenerife, Spain
AP164.S1.1998.D2	113	San Fermín Oeste		Madrid, Spain
AP164.S1.1999.D1	114	Murcia		Murcia, Spain
AP164.S1.1999.D2	115	Museo arqueológico Alicante	Archaeological Museum of Alicante	Alicante, Spain
AP164.S1.1999.D3	116	Paseo marítimo Torrevieja	Waterfront promenade	Torrevieja, Spain
AP164.S1.1999.D4	117	Edificio de servicios generales para la Universidad de Extremadura, Mérida	University of Extremadura service building	Mérida, Spain
AP164.S1.1999.D5	118	Estación Zaragoza	Zaragoza railway station	Zaragoza, Spain
AP164.S1.1999.D6	119	Estudio Gordillo		Villanueva de la Cañada, Spain
AP164.S1.1999.D7	120	Casa Varzavsky		Formentor, Mallorca, Spain
AP164.S1.1999.D8	121	Poblenou, Cerdà Barcelona		Barcelona, Spain
AP164.S1.1999.D9	122	Estación maritima de Salerno	Port terminal	Salerno, Italy
AP164.S1.1999.D10	123	El Mirador: torre mixta en la bahía de Algeciras	El Mirador: mixed-used tower on the Bay of Gibraltar	Algeciras, Spain
AP164.S1.2000.D1	125	Instituto en Almería	Secondary school	Almería, Spain
AP164.S1.2000.D2	126	Torrelodones		Torrelodones, Madrid, Spain
AP164.S1.2000.D3	127	Pabellón de gimnasia en el parque del Retiro	Gymnastics pavilion in Retiro Park	Madrid, Spain
AP164.S1.2000.D4	128	Jardines Valdemingómez	Valdemingómez gardens	Madrid, Spain
AP164.S1.2000.D5	129 157 166–168	Es Pil·lari		Palma de Mallorca, Spain
AP164.S1.2000.D6	130	Planta de biometanización y compostaje de residuos urbanos, Pinto	Biomethanation and composting plant	Pinto, Spain
AP164.S1.2000.D7	131	Einsteinet, edificio de oficinas y show-room	Einsteinet, office building and showroom	Hamburg, Germany
AP164.S1.2000.D8	132	Colegios Magenta		
AP164.S1.2000.D8.SD1	132	Centro de enseñanza secundaria obligatoria de Solana de los Barros	Secondary school	Solana de los Barros, Badajoz, Spain
AP164.S1.2000.D8.SD2	132	Centro de enseñanza secundaria obligatoria en Calamonte	Secondary school	Calamonte, Badajoz, Spain
AP164.S1.2000.D8.SD3	132	Centro de enseñanza secundaria obligatoria de Valverde de Leganés	Secondary school	Valverde de Leganés, Badajoz, Spain

Project	Nr.	Spanish title	English title	Location
AP164.S1.2000.D8.SD4	132	Centro de enseñanza secundaria obligatoria de Fuente de Cantos, Spain	Secondary school	Fuente de Cantos, Badajoz, Spain
AP164.S1.2000.D9	133	Barcelona Forum 2004		Sant Adrià de Besòs, Barcelona, Spain
AP164.S1.2000.D9.SD1	133.1 133.2 133.6–11	Parque litoral Nord-est	Nord-est coast park, Barcelona Forum 2004	Sant Adrià de Besòs, Barcelona, Spain
AP164.S1.2000.D9.SD2	133.3 133–4 133–5	Edificio de oficinas y planta integral de RSU	Ecoparc del Mediterrani recycling plant and offices	Sant Adrià de Besòs, Barcelona, Spain
AP164.S1.2000.D10	134	Casa Mora		Cádiz, Spain
AP164.S1.2001.D1	136	Complejo de justicia, Aachen	Justice complex	Aachen, Germany
AP164.S1.2001.D2	137	Torre Barcelona		Barcelona, Spain
AP164.S1.2001.D3	138	Casa Marina Collazo		Las Rozas de Madrid, Spain
AP164.S1.2001.D4	139	Southbank Londres	South Bank	London, United Kingdom
AP164.S1.2001.D5	140	Loewe		Madrid, Spain
AP164.S1.2001.D6	141	Fundación Helga de Alvear		Cáceres, Spain
AP164.S1.2001.D7	142	Plaza y torre Woermann, Las Palmas	Woermann Plaza and Tower	Las Palmas de Gran Canaria, Spain
AP164.S1.2001.D8	143	Ciudad Real		Ciudad Real, Spain
AP164.S1.2001.D9	144	Centro de enseñanza secundaria	Secondary school	Tiétar, Cáceres, Spain
AP164.S1.2002.D1	145	Oficinas y show-rooms Área, Madrid	Offices and showrooms	Madrid, Spain
AP164.S1.2002.D2	146	Torres mixtas bioclimáticas en el Humedal de Salburua, Vitoria	Environmental mixed-use towers in the Salburua wetlands	Vitoria-Gasteiz, Spain
AP164.S1.2002.D3	147	Parque Cristina Enea	Cristina Enea Park	San Sebastián, Spain
AP164.S1.2002.D4	148	Parque Igara	Igara Park	San Sebastián, Spain
AP164.S1.2002.D5	149	Centro de reciclaje y revaloración	Recycling centre	Logroño, Spain
AP164.S1.2002.D6	150	Recualificación de la planta de compostaje La Paloma	Renovation of La Paloma Composting Plant	Valdemingómez, Madrid, Spain
AP164.S1.2002.D7	151	Casa Gil Peña		Alcobendas, Spain
AP164.S1.2002.D8	n/a	10JH, Sant Andreu viviendas para jóvenes	Youth housing in Sant Andreu	Barcelona, Spain
AP164.S1.2002.D8.SD1	152.1	10JH, Sant Andreu viviendas para jóvenes, manzana 1 y 2	Youth housing in Sant Andreu, blocks 1 and 2	Barcelona, Spain
AP164.S1.2002.D8.SD1	152.2	10JH, Sant Andreu viviendas para jóvenes, manzana 3	Youth housing in Sant Andreu, block 3	Barcelona, Spain
AP164.S1.2002.D9	153	Operación Chamartin	Chamartin operation	Madrid, Spain
AP164.S1.2002.D10	154	Orfila, viviendas, local y garaje	Orfila apartments, retail space and garage	Madrid, Spain
AP164.S1.2002.D11	155	Hotel Toyo, Almería		Almería, Spain
AP164.S1.2002.D12	156	HiperCatalunya		Catalonia, Spain
AP164.S1.2002.D13	158	Centro de Cirugía de Mínima Invasión, Cáceres	Minimally Invasive Surgery Centre	Cáceres, Spain
AP164.S1.2002.D14	159	Fira 2000, Barcelona		Barcelona, Spain
AP164.S1.2002.D15	160	Ordenación ferrocarril Almería	Planning proposal for railway area	Almería, Spain
AP164.S1.2003.D1	161	New Museum de Arte Contemporáneo, New York	New Museum of Contemporary Art	New York, United States
AP164.S1.2003.D2	162	Sociópolis, Valencia		Valencia, Spain
AP164.S1.2003.D3	163	Ordenación de la ribera del arroyo Trejo-Guadalporcún, Setenil de las Bodegas	Planning proposal for the Trejo-Guadalporcún riverside	Setenil de las Bodegas, Cádiz, Spain
AP164.S1.2003.D4	164	Casa Luna, Cantagua		Cantagua, Chile
AP164.S1.2003.D5	165	Sagüés	Sagüés: the gates of Ulía Park	San Sebastián, Spain
AP164.S1.2003.D6	169	Reordenación del Max-Reinhardt Platz, Salzburg	Planning proposal for Max-Reinhardt-Platz	Salzburg, Austria
AP164.S1.2003.D7	170	Biblioteca de México	National Library of Mexico	Mexico City, Mexico
AP164.S1.2003.D8	171	Galería de Pepe Cobo		Madrid, Spain
AP164.S1.2003.D9	172	Metro de Málaga	Málaga metro	Málaga, Spain
AP164.S1.2003.D10	173	Urbanización del sector La Lastra, León	La Lastra master plan	León, Spain
AP164.S1.2003.D11	174	Helipuerto Forum	Forum heliport	Barcelona, Spain
AP164.S1.2003.D12	175	The Collection building, Miami		Miami, United States
AP164.S1.2003.D13	176	Laboratorios de ciencias moleculares para la Universidad de Puerto Rico	Molecular sciences laboratories for the University of Puerto Rico	San Juan, Puerto Rico
AP164.S1.2004.D1	179	Renovación de la fachada del Saint-Georges Centre, Geneva	Renovation of the facade of the Saint-Georges Centre	Geneva, Switzerland
AP164.S1.2004.D2	180	Edificio de equipamiento, Alcalá de Henares	Library and botanical garden	Alcalá de Henares, Spain
AP164.S1.2004.D3	181	Plan de ordenación territorial, Costa del Sol	Regional master plan	Costa del Sol, Spain

Project	Nr.	Spanish title	English title	Location
AP164.S1.2004.D4	182	Polideportivo	Sports hall	Molina de Segura, Murcia, Spain
AP164.S1.2004.D5	183	Alcorque para León	Tree grating	León, Spain
AP164.S1.2004.D6	184	Puentes de León		León, Spain
AP164.S1.2004.D7	185	Pepe Cobo II, galería de arte	Pepe Cobo II, art gallery	Madrid, Spain
AP164.S1.2004.D8	186	DeCoro: decoración urbana	DeCoro: urban decoration	
AP164.S1.2004.D9	187	EPFL learning center, Lausanne		Lausanne, Switzerland
AP164.S1.2004.D10	188	Integración del ferrocarril, Logroño	Integration of the railway in Logroño	Logroño, Spain
AP164.S1.2004.D11	189	Shujiajiao new canal town		Shanghai, China
AP164.S1.2004.D12	190	Filmoteca de Cataluña	Filmoteca de Catalunya	Barcelona, Spain
AP164.S1.2004.D13	191	Palacio de congresos y ferial internacional de León	International convention centre	León, Spain
AP164.S1.2004.D14	195	APTM Construmat	APTM: proposal for a basic apartment	Barcelona, Spain
AP164.S1.2004.D15	196	Colegio en Puigpunyent	School	Puigpunyent, Mallorca, Spain
AP164.S1.2005.D1	197	Tour TSR, Geneva	Renovation of the TSR Tower	Geneva, Switzerland
AP164.S1.2005.D2	199	Proyecto en México-Pedregal	Project in Mexico-Pedregal	Mexico City, Mexico
AP164.S1.2005.D3	201	Colina artificial, International Architecture Biennale Rotterdam	The Artificial Hill, International Architecture Biennale Rotterdam	Leeuwarden, Netherlands
AP164.S1.2005.D4	205	CEARD de lanzamiento y atletismo, León	Athletic training centre	León, Spain
AP164.S1.2005.D5	206	Casa Vadillo		
AP164.S1.2005.D6	209	M-30: parque lineal del río Manzanares	M-30: park along the Manzanares River	Madrid, Spain
AP164.S1.2005.D7	211	Villa en Forest Forever, Beijing	Villa in Forest Forever	Beijing, China
AP164.S1.2005.D8	n/a	Marsella	Marseille	Marseille, France
AP164.S1.2005.D9	212	Orange County Great Park		Orange County, California, United States
AP164.S1.2006.D2	215	Concurso Vitoria Ibaialde	Vitoria Ibaialde Competition	Vitoria-Gasteiz, Spain
AP164.S1.2006.D1	216	Hecansa		Las Palmas de Gran Canaria, Spain
AP164.S1.2005.D10	n/a	Palast der Republik, Berlin		Berlin, Germany

AP164: Ábalos&Herreros selected by Kersten Geers and David Van Severen, Juan José Castellón González, Florian Idenburg and Jing Liu, with an interpretation in photographs by Stefano Graziani presents the results of the 2014–2015 Out of the Box research program on the Ábalos&Herreros archive. It is published by the Canadian Centre for Architecture and Park Books.

Project direction:
Giovanna Borasi

Researchers and guest curators:
Kersten Geers and David Van Severen,
Juan José Castellón González,
Florian Idenburg and Jing Liu

Invited artist:
Stefano Graziani

Editor-in-charge:
Andrew Goodhouse

Book design:
NODE Berlin Oslo

Exhibition graphic design and booklet design:
Jonathan Hares

Exhibition research and curatorial coordination:
Simon Pennec and Rebecca Taylor with Greg Barton and Alice Haddad

Exhibition design development:
Sébastien Larivière

Spanish to English translation:
Elaine Fradley

CCA photography:
Michel Boulet, Mathieu Gagnon

Exhibition videos:
Adam Thompson

Lithography:
Norbert Dietsche, Perfektbild

Rights and reproductions:
Marc Pitre

Cataloguing of the archive:
Jennifer Préfontaine

Special thanks to Serge Rompza and Jonathan Hares for their expertise, criticism and creativity in the design of the book and the series of exhibitions respectively; to Emilio Tuñón for generously granting permission to reproduce the 1993 issue of CIRCO presented in the first pages of the book; to Moisés Puente and Jesús Vassallo for their advice; to Katharina Tauer for ensuring the implementation of the book design; to Molly Minot Hubley (SO – IL) for her contribution to the development of Landscapes of the Hyperreal and to www.carpet-printing.com for the fabrication of the carpet.

All material with an AP164 number is part of the Ábalos&Herreros archive, Centre Canadien d'Architecture / Canadian Centre for Architecture, Montreal
Gift of Iñaki Ábalos and Juan Herreros

All works by Ábalos&Herreros
© Iñaki Ábalos and Juan Herreros

Every reasonable attempt has been made to appropriately credit material appearing in this publication. Errors and omissions will be corrected in subsequent reprints.

"Una conversación" originally published in CIRCO 9 (1993). Courtesy CIRCO M.R.T. coop

Proofs of Relevance is a gift of the artist and part of the CCA collection. © Stefano Graziani

Lewis Baltz photographs are part of the CCA collection. © Successors of Lewis Baltz

Photo credits

pp. 14–15
View of an administrative building for the Spanish Ministry of the Interior. Photograph by Manolo Laguillo

p. 68
View of the Brunswick Building.
From Myron Goldsmith, *Buildings and Concepts* (New York: Rizzoli, 1987), 100. Photograph by Bill Eduardo Torroja for Hedrich-Blessing

Plan and interior views of the Rockefeller Center. Top: From Sigfried Giedion, *Space, Time and Architecture* (Cambridge, MA: Harvard University Press, 1941), 774. Bottom: From Ernst Erik Pfannschmidt, *Metallmöbel* (Stuttgart: Julius Hoffmann Verlag, 1962), 111

p. 69
Plan of Osram GmbH Administration Building.
From E. D. Mills, *The Changing Workplace: The Design of Factories and Offices Related To Modern Technology* (London: George Godwin Limited, 1972), 97. Drawing by Walter Henn, architects

p. 72
View of Asahi Superdry Hall.
From *Japan Architecture*, Winter 1990

p. 134
Views showing the beachfront and isthmus of Las Palmas de Gran Canaria, and sketches of the design of the Woermann Plaza and Tower. Photograph at bottom by José Hevia

p. 136
Page layout showing floor plans, section and partial views of the Woermann Tower. Photograph at bottom by José Hevia

p. 156
View of the Eldorado. Photograph by Diego Torres Silvestre

View of Marina City. From Carl W. Condit, *American Building: Materials and Techniques from the First Colonial Settlements to the Present* (Chicago: University of Chicago Press, 1982), 280. Photograph by Richard Nickel

p. 157
View of prototypes of spatial structures by Robert Le Ricolais. From *Zodiac*, no. 22 (1973): 4, 67. Photographs by Peter McCleary

Tower of the Winds. From Terrence Riley, *Light Construction* (New York: Museum of Modern Art, 1995), 133. Photograph by Shinkenchiku-Sha

The CCA is an international research centre and museum founded on the conviction that architecture is a public concern. Based on its extensive collection, exhibitions, programs and research opportunities the CCA is a leading voice in advancing knowledge, promoting public understanding and widening thought and debate on architecture, its history, theory, practice and role in society today.

CCA Board of Trustees
Phyllis Lambert, Founding Director Emeritus; Bruce Kuwabara, Chair; Pierre-André Themens, Vice-Chair; Guido Beltramini; Stephen R. Bronfman; Barry Campbell; Michael Conforti; Timur Galen; Normand Grégoire; Isabelle Jomphe; Sylvia Lavin; Frederick Lowy; Gerald Sheff; Mirko Zardini.
Honorary members: Serge Joyal, Warren Simpson

The CCA gratefully acknowledges the generous support of the Ministère de la Culture et des Communications, the Canada Council for the Arts and the Conseil des arts de Montréal.

© 2016 Canadian Centre for Architecture and Park Books AG, Zurich
All rights reserved under international copyright conventions.

Legal depot: February 2016

Printed and bound in Germany
First edition

CCA edition:
ISBN 978-1-927071-30-4
Canadian Centre for Architecture
1920 rue Baile
Montréal, Québec
Canada H3H 2S6
www.cca.qc.ca

Trade edition:
ISBN 978-3-03860-006-0
Park Books
Niederdorfstrasse 54
8001 Zürich
Switzerland
www.park-books.com

Also issued in Spanish by the Canadian Centre for Architecture and Park Books

Bibliothèque et Archives nationales du Québec and Library and Archives Canada cataloguing in publication

Main entry under title:
AP164: Ábalos & Herreros

Texts in English and Spanish.
ISBN 978-1-927071-30-4

1. Ábalos & Herreros. 2. Architecture – Spain – History – 20th century. 3. Architects – Spain – Biography. I. Geers, Kersten, 1975–. II. Severen, David van, 1978–. III. Castellón González, Juan José. IV. Idenburg, Florian, 1975–. V. Liu, Jing, 1980–. VI. Graziani, Stefano. VII. Canadian Centre for Architecture. VIII. Titre: Ábalos & Herreros.

NA1313.A22A85 2016
790.92'2
C2016-940346-7